AF559904

TEXTBOOK OF SOIL CHEMISTRY

TEXTBOOK
OF
SOIL CHEMISTRY

By

Dr. Lata Bhattacharya

Professor

School of Studies in Zoology & Biotechnology

Vikram University

Ujjain (M.P.)

(India)

DISCOVERY PUBLISHING HOUSE PVT. LTD.

NEW DELHI-110 002

Reprinted - 2019

First Published - 2010

ISBN: 978-81-8356-580-6

Textbok of Soil Chemistry

Published by:

DISCOVERY PUBLISHING HOUSE PVT. LTD.
4383/4B, Ansari Road, Darya Ganj
New Delhi-110 002 (India)
Phone: +91-11-23279245, 43596064-65
Fax: +91-11-23253475
E-mail: discoverypublishinghouse@gmail.com
sales@discoverypublishinggroup.com
web: www.discoverypublishinggroup.com

Printed at:
Infinity Imaging Systems
Delhi

Preface

Until the late 1960s, soil chemistry focused primarily on chemical reactions in the soil that contribute to pedogenesis or that affect plant growth. Since then concerns have grown about environmental pollution, organic and inorganic soil contamination and potential ecological health and environmental health risks. Consequently, the emphasis in soil chemistry has shifted from pedology and agricultural soil science to an emphasis on environmental soil science.

A knowledge of environmental soil chemistry is paramount to predicting the fate, mobility and potential toxicity of contaminants in the environment. The vast majority of environmental contaminants are initially released to the soil. Once a chemical is exposed to the soil environment a myriad of chemical reactions can occur that may increase/decrease contaminant toxicity. These reactions include adsorption/desorption, precipitation, polymerization, dissolution, complexation, and oxidation/reduction. These reactions are often disregarded by scientists and engineers involved with environmental remediation. Understanding these processes enable us to better predict the fate and toxicity of contaminants and provide the knowledge to develop scientifically correct, and cost-effective remediation strategies.

Soil is the naturally occurring, unconsolidated or loose covering on the Earth's surface. Soil is made up of broken rock particles that have been altered by chemical and environmental conditions, affected by processes such as weathering and erosion. Soil is different from its parent rock(s) source(s), altered by interactions between the lithosphere, hydrosphere, atmosphere, and the biosphere. It is a mixture of mineral and organic constituents that are in solid, gaseous and aqueous states. Soil particles pack loosely, forming a soil structure filled with pore spaces. These pores contain sol solution (liquid) and air (gas). Accordingly, soils are often treated as a three-state system. Most soils have a density between 1 and 2, and weigh between 60 and 120 pounds per cubic foot. Soil is also known as earth: it is the substance from which our planet takes its name.

–Author

Contents

CHAPTER–1

Introduction

Soil chemistry studies the chemical characteristics of soil. Soil chemistry is affected by mineral composition, organic matter and environmental factors. Until the late 1960s, soil chemistry focused primarily on chemical reactions in the soil that contribute to pedogenesis or that affect plant growth. Since then concerns have grown about environmental pollution, organic and inorganic soil contamination and potential ecological health and environmèntal health risks. Consequently, the emphasis in soil chemistry has shifted from pedology and agricultural soil science to an emphasis on environmental soil science.

A knowledge of environmental soil chemistry is paramount to predicting the fate, mobility and potential toxicity of contaminants in the environment. The vast majority of environmental contaminants are initially released to the soil. Once a chemical is exposed to the soil environment a myriad of chemical reactions can occur that may increase/decrease contaminant toxicity. These reactions include adsorption/desorption, precipitation, polymerization, dissolution, complexation, and oxidation/reduction. These reactions are often disregarded by scientists and engineers involved with environmental remediation. Understanding these processes enable us to better predict the fate and toxicity of contaminants and provide the knowledge to develop scientifically correct, and cost-effective remediation strategies.

Soil is the naturally occurring, unconsolidated or loose covering on the Earth's surface. Soil is made up of broken rock particles that have been altered by chemical and environmental conditions, affected by processes such as weathering and erosion. Soil is different from its parent rock(s) source(s), altered by interactions between the lithosphere, hydrosphere, atmosphere, and the biosphere. It is a mixture of mineral and organic constituents that are in solid, gaseous and aqueous states. Soil particles pack loosely, forming a soil structure filled with pore spaces. These pores contain sol solution (liquid) and air (gas). Accordingly, soils are often treated as a three state system. Most soils have a density between 1 and 2, and weigh between 60 and 120 pounds per cubic foot. Soil is also known as earth: it is the substance from which our planet takes its name.

Characteristics

Soil colour is the first impression one has when viewing soil. Striking colours and contrasting patterns are especially memorable. The Red River in Louisiana carries sediment eroded from extensive reddish soils like Port Silt Loam in Oklahoma. Soil colour results from chemical and biological weathering. As the primary minerals in parent material weather, the elements combine into new and colourful compounds. Iron forms secondary minerals with a yellow or red colour; organic matter decomposes into brown compounds; and manganese, sulfur and nitrogen can form black mineral deposits

Soil structure is the arrangement of soil particles into aggregates. These may have various shapes, sizes and degrees of development or expression

Soil texture refers to sand, silt and clay composition. Sand and silt are the product of physical weathering while soil is the product of chemical weathering. Soil content is particularly influential on soil behaviour due to a high retention capacity for nutrients and water.

The electrical resistivity of soil can affect the rate of galvanic corrosion of metallic structures in contact with it. Higher moister content or increased electrolyte concentration can lower the resistivity and thereby increase the rate of corrosion. Soil resistivity values typically range from about 2 to 1000 O·m, but more extreme values are not unusual.

Formation

Soil formation, or pedogenesis, is the combined effect of physical, chemical, biological, and anthropogenic processes on soil parent material resulting in the formation of soil horizons. Soil is always changing. The long periods over which change occurs and the multiple influences of change mean that simple soils are rare. While soil can achieve relative stability in properties for extended periods of time, the soil life cycle ultimately ends in soil conditions that leave it vulnerable to erosion. Little of the soil composition of the earth is older than Tertiary and most no older than Pleistocene Despite the inevitability of soils retrogression and degradation, most soil cycles are long and productive. How the soil "life" cycle proceeds is influenced by at least five classic soil forming factors: regional climate, biotic potential, topography, parent material, and the passage of time. An example of soil development from bare rock occurs on recent lava flows in warm regions under heavy and very frequent rainfall. In such climates plants become established very quickly on basaltic lava, even though there is very little organic material. The plants are supported by the porous rock becoming filled with nutrient bearing water, for example carrying dissolved bird droppings or guano. The developing plant roots themselves gradually break up the porous lava and organic matter soon accumulates. But even before it does, the predominantly porous broken lava in which the plant roots grow can be considered a soil.

Organic Matter

Most living things found in soils, including plants, insects, bacteria and fungi, are dependent on organic matter for nutrients and energy. Soils often have varying degrees of organic compounds in different states of decomposition. Many soils, including desert and rocky-gravel soils, have no or little organic matter; while soils, such as peat (Histosols), that are all organic matter are infertile.

Humus

Humus refers to organic matter that has decomposed to a point were it is resistant to further breakdown or alteration. Humus typically forms from plant residues like foliage, stems and roots. After death, these plant residues begin to decay, starting the formation of humus. Humus formation involves changes within the soil and plant residue, there is a reduction of water soluble constituents including cellulose and hemicellulose; as the residues are deposited and break down, lignin and lignin complexes accumulate within the soil; as microorganisms live and feed on the decaying plant matter, an increase in proteins occurs.

Lignin is resistant to breakdown and accumulates within the soil, it also chemically reacts with amino acids which add to its resistance to decomposition, including enzymatic decomposition by microbes. Fats and waxes from plant matter have some resistance to decomposition and persist in soils for a while. Proteins normally decompose readily but when bound to clay particles they become more resistant to decomposition, clay particles also absorb enzymes that would break down proteins, thus clay soils often have higher organic contents that persist longer than soils without clay. The addition of organic matter to clay soils, can render the organic matter and any added nutrients inaccessible to plants and microbes for many years, since they can bind strongly to the clay.

Humus formation is a processes dependent on the amount of plant material added each year and the type of base soil; both are affected by climate and the type of microorganisms present. Soils with humus can vary in nitrogen content but have 3 to 6 per cent nitrogen typically; humus as a reserve of nitrogen and phosphorus, is a vital component effecting soil fertility. Humus also adsorbs water, acting as a moisture reserve, that plants can utilize; it also expands and shrinks between dry and wet states, providing pore spaces. Humus is less stable than other soil constituents, because it is affected by microbial decomposition, and over time its concentration decreases without the addition of new organic matter.

Climate and Organics

The production and accumulation, or degradation, of organic matter and humus is greatly depended on climate conditions. Temperature and soil moisture are major factors in the formation or degradation of humus and the formation of organic soils. Soils high in organic matter tend to form under wet conditions and/or were there is enough precipitation to sustain thick vegetation

In Nature

Biogeography is the study of special variations in biological communities. Soils are restricting factor as to what plants can grow in which environments. Soil scientists survey soils in the hope of understanding controls as to what vegetation can and will grow in a particular location.

Geologists also have a particular interest in the patterns of soil on the surface of the earth. Soil texture, colour and chemistry often reflect the underlying geologic parent material and soil types often change at geologic unit boundaries. Buried paleosols mark previous land surfaces and record climatic conditions from previous eras. Geologists use this paleopedological record to understand the ecological relationships in past ecosystems. According to the theory of biorhexistasy, prolonged conditions conducive to forming deep, weathered soils result in increasing ocean salinity and the formation of limestone.

Geologists use soil profile features to establish the duration of surface stability in the context of geologic faults or slope stability. An offset subsoil horizon indicates rupture during soil formation and the degree of subsequent subsoil formation is relied upon to establish time since rupture.

Soil examined in shovel test pits is used by archaeologists for relative dating based on stratigraphy (as opposed to absolute dating). What is considered most typical is to use soil profile features to determine the maximum reasonable pit depth than needs to be examined for archaeological evidence in the interest of cultural resources management.

Soils altered or formed by man (anthropic and anthropogenic soils) are also of interest to archaeologists.

Uses

Soil is used in agriculture, where it serves as the primary nutrient base for the plants. The types of soil used in agriculture (among other things, such as the purported level of moisture in the soil) vary with respect to the species of plants that are cultivated.

Soil material is a critical component in the mining and construction industries. Soil serves as a foundation for most construction projects. Massive volumes of soil can be involved in surface mining, road building, and dam construction. Earth sheltering is the architectural practice of using soil for external thermal mass against building walls.

Soil resources are critical to the environment, as well as to food and fiber production. Soil provides minerals and water to plants. Soil absorbs rainwater and releases it later thus preventing floods and drought. Soil cleans the water as it percolates. Soil is the habitat for many organisms.

Waste management often has a soil component. Septic drain fields treat septic tank effluent using aerobic soil processes. Landfills use soil for daily cover.

Organic soils, especially peat, serve as a significant fuel resource.

Both humans in many cultures and animals occasionally eat soil.

Soils play an important role in filtrating and purifying water. After coming down as precipitation, much of the rain water is percolated through the many horizons of a soil profile and renamed as groundwater. As the water moves through different areas such as wetlands, forests, and riparian zones many pollutants are removed. Pollutants such as viruses, oils, metals, excess nutrients, and sediments are filtered out by the soil and surrounding organisms.

Riparian zones act as living filters which absorb and take in excess nutrients and pollutants brought in from runoff, rainfall, and surrounding areas. These natural filtration systems are important in purifying our drinking water as much as possible before it reaches treatment plants to reduce the cost of that treatment and to minimize the amount of chemicals added in order to make it drinkable.

Degradation

Land degradation is a human induced or natural process which impairs the capacity of land to function. Soils are the critical component in land degradation when it involves acidification, contamination, desertification, erosion, or salination.

While soil acidification of alkaline soils is beneficial, it degrades land when soil acidity lowers crop productivity and increases soil vulnerability to contamination and erosion. Soils are often initially acid because their parent materials were acid and initially low in the basic cations (calcium, magnesium, potassium, and sodium). Acidification occurs when these elements are removed from the soil profile by normal rainfall or the harvesting of crops. Soil acidification is accelerated by the use of acid-forming nitrogenous fertilizers and by the effects of acid precipitation.

Soil contamination at low levels are often within soil capacity to treat and assimilate. Many waste treatment processes rely on this treatment capacity. Exceeding treatment capacity can damage soil biota and limit soil function. Derelict soils occur where industrial contamination or other development activity damages the soil to such a degree that the land cannot be used safely or productively. Remediation of derelict soil uses principles of geology, physics, chemistry, and biology to degrade, attenuate, isolate, or remove soil contaminants and to restore soil functions and values. Techniques include leaching, air sparging, chemical amendments, phytoremediation, bioremediation, and natural attenuation.

Desertification is an environmental process of ecosystem degradation in arid and semi-arid regions, or as a result of human activity. It is a common misconception that droughts cause desertification. Droughts are common in arid and semiarid lands. Well-managed lands can recover from drought when the rains return. Soil management tools include maintaining soil nutrient and organic matter levels, reduced tillage and increased cover. These help to control erosion and maintain productivity during periods when moisture is available. Continued land abuse during droughts, however, increases land degradation. Increased population and livestock pressure on marginal lands accelerates desertification.

Soil erosional loss is caused by wind, water, ice, movement in response to gravity. Although the processes may be simultaneous, erosion is distinguished from weathering. Erosion is an intrinsic natural process, but in many places it is increased by human land use. Poor land use practices include deforestation, overgrazing, and improper construction activity. Improved management can limit erosion using techniques like limiting disturbance during construction, avoiding construction during erosion prone periods, intercepting runoff, terrace-building, use of erosion suppressing cover materials and planting trees or other soil binding plants.

A serious and long-running water erosion problem is in China, on the middle reaches of the Yellow River and the upper reaches of the Yangtze River. From the Yellow River, over 1.6 billion tons of sediment flow each year into the ocean. The sediment originates primarily from water erosion (Gully erosion) in the Loess Plateau region of northwest China.

Soil piping is a particular form of soil erosion that occurs below the soil surface. It is associated with levee and dam failure as well as sink hole formation. Turbulent flow removes soil starting from the mouth of the seep flow and subsoil erosion advances upgradient. The term sand boil is used to describe the appearance of the discharging end of an active soil pipe.

Soil salination is the accumulation of free salts to such an extent that it leads to degradation of soils and vegetation. Consequences include corrosion damage, reduced plant growth, erosion due to loss of plant cover and soil structure, and water quality problems due to sedimentation. Salination occurs due to a combination of natural and human caused processes. Aridic conditions favor salt accumulation. This is especially apparent when soil parent material is saline. Irrigation of arid lands is especially problematic. All irrigation water has some level of salinity. Irrigation, especially when it involves leakage from canals, often raise the underlying water table. Rapid salination occurs when the land surface is within the capillary fringe of saline groundwater. Salinity control involves flushing with higher levels of applied water in combination with tile drainage.

CHAPTER–2

Soil pH

INTRODUCTION

The pH is a measure of the acidity or alkalinity of a solution. An acid solution has a pH value less than 7. While a basic solution always has a pH larger than 7, an alkaline solution (i.e. a solution with positive acid neutralizing capacity) does not necessarily have a pH larger than 7. For details on the relation between pH and ANC, see acid neutralizing capacity.

Soil pH is an important consideration for farmers and gardeners for several reasons:

- Many plants and soil life forms prefer either alkaline or acidic conditions.
- Some diseases tend to thrive when the soil is alkaline or acidic.
- The pH can affect the availability of nutrients in the soil.
- Nutrient availability in relation to soil pH.

The majority of food crops prefer a neutral or slightly acidic soil. Some plants however prefer more acidic (e.g., potatoes, strawberries) or alkaline (brassicas) conditions.

During the acidification process the decrease in pH results in a release of positively charged ions (cations) from the cation exchange surfaces (organic matter and clay minerals). In the short term acidification thus increases the concentration of potassium (K), magnesium (Mg) and calcium (Ca) in soil solution. Once the cation exchange surface has become depleted of these ions, however, the concentration in soil solution can be quite low and is largely determined by the weathering rate. The weathering rate in turn is dependent on such things as mineralogy (e.g. presence of easily weathered minerals), surface area (i.e. the soil texture), soil moisture (i.e. how large a fraction of the mineral surface area that is wet), pH, concentration of base cations such as Ca, Mg and K as well as concentration of aluminium. The amount of plant available nutrients is a much more difficult issue than soil solution concentrations. The term plant available nutrients usually include pools other than soil solution but which are supposed to replenish soil solution pretty fast e.g. through cation exchange. One reason for including such pools is the plants capability of releasing organic acids which increase the total soil solution concentration of some cation nutrients that are important for the plant.

It is thus important to realize that there exists no simple relation between soil solution concentration of Ca, Mg and K and reasonable pH-values. The reason for this is that Ca, Mg and K are base cations, i.e. cations of strong bases and strong bases are fully dissociated at the pH-ranges occurring in most natural waters. However, as the soil solution pH is dependent on mineral weathering and mineral weathering increase pH by releasing Ca, Mg and K a soil which is rich in easily weatherable minerals tends to have both a higher pH and higher soil solution concentration of Ca, Mg and K. On the other hand deposition of sulphate, nitrate and to some extent ammonia decrease pH of soil solution essentially without affecting Ca, Mg and K concentrations whereas deposition of sea salt increases Ca, Mg and K concentrations without having much of an effect on soil solution.

pH

When interpreting soil solution pH values it is essential to take into account the method by which pH has been measured. Depending on whether or not the water has been equilibrated with ambient CO_2 pressure or not the pH reported from the same site may be either high or low. This is simply because the carbon dioxide pressure deep down in the soil might be 10–20 times higher than the ambient pressure due to decomposition of organic material. The higher carbon dioxide pressure result in more carbonic acid and hence a lower pH. Furthermore, soil solution can be extracted from the soil in many ways, e.g. by lysimeters, zero-tension lysimeters, centrifugation, extraction with $CaCl_2$, overhead shaking of soil sample with added water, etc. The $CaCl_2$ extraction method do not give the actual soil solution pH but rather a mix between soil solution pH and what is easily available e.g. through cation exchange. Also when mixing soil samples with water and using overhead shakers (or similar) the result is a mix between actual soil solution and cation exchange, although the hope is that the extracted water will be similar to the actual soil solution in most respects. If centrifugation or pressurised lysimeters are used, care must be taken that the extracted water do not include water that is not readily available (think wilting point and crystal water). Naturally, taking a sample introduces a disturbance of the system, which can e.g. result in a change in nutrient uptake and decomposition rates (e.g. due to cutting of fine roots when placing the lysimeter).

Many nutrient cations such as zinc (Zn_2^+), aluminium (Al_3^+), iron (Fe_2^+), copper (Cu_2^+), cobalt (Co_2^+), and manganese (Mn_2^+) are soluble and available for uptake by plants below pH 5.0, although their availability can be excessive and thus toxic in more acidic conditions. In more alkaline conditions they are less available, and symptoms of nutrient deficiency may result, including thin plant stems, yellowing (chlorosis) or mottling of leaves, and slow or stunted growth.

pH levels also affect the complex interactions among soil chemicals. Phosphorus (P) for example requires a pH between 6.0 and 7.0 and becomes chemically immobile outside this range, forming insoluble compounds with iron (Fe) and aluminium (Al) in acid soils and with calcium (Ca) in calcareous soils.

How is Acidic Soil Formed

To understand how acid soils are formed, take a simple walk through a woodland. Rainfall filters through trees and into the ground, where it dissolves limestone sediment and other alkaline minerals that help neutralize soil acidity. The woodland floor is carpeted in needles of conifers, leaves of hardwood trees, and other dead plant matter, most of which increase soil acidity as they decompose. Unless this woodland is on top of a huge deposit of alkaline material such as limestone or serpentine, the soil will tend to be acid.

Soils and Acidity

Under conditions in which rainfall exceeds evapo-transpiration (leaching) during most of the year, the basic soil cations (Ca, Mg, K) are gradually depleted and replaced with cations held in colloidal soil reserves, leading to soil acidity. Clay soils often contain Fe and hydroxy Al, which affect the retention and availability of fertilizer cations and anions in acidic soils.

Soil acidification may also occur by addition of hydrogen, due to decomposition of organic matter, acid-forming fertilizers, and exchange of basic cations for H^+ by the roots.

Soil acidity is reduced by volatilization and denitrification of nitrogen. Under flooded conditions, the soil pH value increases. In addition, the following nitrate fertilizers-calcium nitrate, magnesium nitrate, potassium nitrate and sodium nitrate—also increase the soil pH value.

Some alkaline soils have Calcium in the form of limestone that is not chemically available to plants. In this case sulphuric acid or Sulphur may be added to reclaim the soil.

Factors Affecting Soil pH

The pH value of a soil is influenced by the kinds of parent materials from which the soil was formed. Soils developed from basic rocks generally have higher pH values than those formed from acid rocks.

Rainfall also affects soil pH. Water passing through the soil leaches basic nutrients such as calcium and magnesium from the soil. They are replaced by acidic elements such as aluminum and iron. For this reason, soils formed under high rainfall conditions are more acidic than those formed under arid (dry) conditions.

Human distractions like pollution alter the pH of soil. Researches have also revealed that soil pH is affected by the vehicular and ongoing traffic. This largely hampers the soil pH and in turn the primary productivity by compacting the soil and decreasing its friability.

Application of fertilizers containing ammonium or urea speeds up the rate at which acidity develops. The decomposition of organic matter also adds to soil acidity.

Soil Life and pH

A pH level of around 6.3-6.8 is also the optimum range preferred by most soil bacteria, although fungi, molds, and anaerobic bacteria have a broader tolerance and tend to multiply at lower pH values. Therefore, more acidic soils tend to be susceptible to souring and putrefaction, rather than undergoing the sweet decay processes associated with the decay of organic matter, which immeasurably benefit the soil. These processes also prefer near-neutral conditions.

pH and Plant Diseases

Many plant diseases are caused or exacerbated by extremes of pH, sometimes because this makes essential nutrients unavailable to crops or because the soil itself is unhealthy. For example, chlorosis of leaf vegetables and potato scab occur in overly alkaline conditions, and acidic soils can cause clubroot in brassicas.

Determining pH

A map of the pH level is a mosaic, varying according to soil crumb structure, on the surface of colloids, and at microsites. The pH also exhibits vertical gradients, tending to be more acidic in surface mulches and alkaline where evaporation, wormcasts, and capillary action draw bases up to the soil surface. It also varies on a macro level depending on factors such as slope, rocks, and vegetation type. Therefore the pH should be measured regularly and at various points within the land in question.

METHODS OF DETERMINING pH INCLUDE

Observation of soil profile. Strongly acidic soils often have poor incorporation of the organic surface layer with the underlying mineral layer. The mineral horizons are distinctively layered in many cases, with a pale eluvial (E) horizon beneath the organic surface; this E is underlain by a darker B horizon in a classic podzol horizon sequence.

Observation of predominant flora. Calcifuge plants (those that prefer an acidic soil) include Erica, Rhododendron and nearly all other Ericaceae species, many Betula (birch), Digitalis (foxgloves), gorse, and Scots Pine. Calcicole (lime loving) plants include Fraxinus (Ash), Honeysuckle (Lonicera), Buddleia, Cornus spp (dogwoods), Lilac(Syringa) and *Clematis* spp.

Observation of symptoms that might indicate acidic or alkaline conditions, such as occurrence of the plant diseases mentioned above or salinisation of alkaline soils. The house hydrangea (*Hydrangea macrophylla*) produces pink flowers at pH values of 6.8 or higher, and blue flowers at pH 6.0 or below.

Use of an inexpensive pH testing kit based on barium sulfate in powdered form, where in a small sample of soil is mixed with water which changes colour according to the acidity/alkalinity.

Use of litmus paper. A small sample of soil is mixed with distilled water, into which a strip of litmus paper is inserted. If the soil is acidic the paper turns red, if alkaline, blue.

Use of a commercially available electronic pH meter, in which a rod is inserted into moistened soil and measures the concentration of hydrogen ions.

ALTERING SOIL pH

The aim when attempting to adjust soil acidity is not so much to neutralise the pH as to replace lost cation nutrients, particularly calcium. This can be achieved by adding limestone to the soil, which is available in various forms.

Agricultural lime (ground limestone or chalk). These are natural forms of calcium carbonate which are extracted in the UK from areas such as the Mendips and Salisbury Plain. This is probably the cheapest form of lime for gardening and agricultural use and can be applied at any time of the year. These forms are slow reacting, thus their effect on soil fertility and plant growth is steady and long lasting. Ground lime should be applied to clay and heavy soils at a rate of about 500 to 1,000 g/m^2 (1 to 2 lb/yd^2 or 4,500 to 9,000 lb/ac).

Quicklime and slaked lime. The former is produced by burning rock limestone in kilns. It is highly caustic and cannot be applied directly to the soil. Quicklime reacts with water to produce slaked, or hydrated, lime, thus quicklime is spread around agricultural land in heaps to absorb rain and atmospheric moisture and form slaked lime, which is then spread on the soil. Quicklime should be applied to heavy clays at a rate of about 400 to 500 g/m^2 (0.75 to 1 lb/yd^2 or 3,600 to 4,500 lb/ac), hydrated lime at 250 to 500 g/m^2 (0.5 to 1 lb/yd^2). However, quicklime and hydrated lime are very fast acting and are not suitable for inclusion in an organic system. Their use is prohibited under the standards of both The Soil Association and the Henry Doubleday Research Association.

Calcium sulfate, also known as gypsum can not be used to amend soil acidity. It is a common myth that gypsum affects soil acidity However, gypsum does reduce aluminum toxicity. Because gypsum is more soluble than alkaline earth carbonates, it is recommended for the treatment of acidic subsoils.

The pH of an alkaline soil is lowered by adding sulphur, iron sulfate or aluminium sulfate, although these tend to be expensive, and the effects short term. Urea, urea phosphate, ammonium nitrate, ammonium phosphates, ammonium sulfate and monopotassium phosphate also lower soil pH.

ACID SULFATE SOIL

Acid sulfate soils are naturally occurring soils, sediments or organic substrates (e.g. peat) that are formed under waterlogged conditions. These soils contain iron sulfide minerals (predominantly as the mineral pyrite) or their oxidation products. In an undisturbed state below the water table, acid sulfate soils are benign. However if the soils are drained, excavated or exposed to air by a lowering of the water table, the sulfides will react with oxygen to form sulfuric acid.

Release of this sulfuric acid from the soil can in turn release iron, aluminium, and other heavy metals (particularly arsenic) within the soil. Once mobilized in this way, the acid and metals can create a variety of adverse impacts: killing vegetation, seeping into and acidifying groundwater and water bodies, killing fish and other aquatic organisms, and degrading concrete and steel structures to the point of failure.

Acid Sulfate Soil Formation

The soils and sediments which are most prone to becoming acid sulfate soils are those which formed within the last 10,000 years, after the last major sea level rise. When the sea level rose and inundated the land, sulfate in the seawater mixed with land sediments containing iron oxides and organic matter Under these anaerobic conditions, lithotrophic bacteria such as Thiobacillus ferrooxidans form iron sulfides (pyrite). Up to a point, warmer temperatures are more favourable conditions for these bacteria, creating a greater potential for formation of iron sulfides. Tropical waterlogged environments, such as mangrove swamps or estuaries, may contrain higher levels of pyrite than those formed in more temperate climates.

The pyrite is stable until it is exposed to air, at which point the pyrite oxidises and produces sulfuric acid. The impacts of acid sulfate soil leachate may persist over a long time, and/or peak seasonally (after dry periods with the first rains). In some areas of Australia, acid sulfate soils that drained 100 years ago are still releasing acid.

Chemical Reaction

When drained, pyrite (FeS_2) containing soils (also called cat-clays) may become extremely acidic ($pH < 4$) due to the oxidation of pyrite into sulfuric acid (H_2SO_4). In its simplest form, this chemical reaction is as follows:

$$2\,FeS_2 + 9\,O_2 + 4\,H_2O \;?\; 8\,H+ + 4\,SO_4 = + 2\,Fe(OH)_3 \text{ (solid)}$$

The product $Fe(OH)_3$, iron (III) hydroxide (orange), precipi-tates as a solid, insoluble mineral by which the alkalinity component is immobilized, while the acidity remains active in the sulfuric acid. The process of acidification is accompanied by the formation of high amounts of aluminium (Al^{+++}, released from clay minerals under influence of the acidity), which are harmful to vegetation. Otheı products of the chemical reaction are:

1. Hydrogen sulfide (H_2S), a smelly gas.
2. Sulfur (S), a yellow solid.
3. Iron(II) sulfide (FeS), a black/gray/blue solid.
4. Haematite (Fe_2O_3), a red solid.
5. Goethite (FeO.OH), a brown mineral.
6. Schwertmannite a brown mineral.
7. Iron compounds (e.g. jarosite).
8. H-Clay (hydrogen clay, with a large fraction of adsorbed H+ ions, a stable mineral, but poor in nutri-ents).

The iron can be present in bivalent and trivalent forms (Fe^{++}, the ferro ion, and Fe^{+++}, the ferri ion respect-ively). The ferro form is soluble, whereas the ferri form is not. The more oxidized the soil becomes, the more the ferri forms will dominate. Acid sulfate soils exhibit an array of colours ranging from black, brown, blue-gray, red, orange and yellow. The hydrogen clay can be improved by admitting sea water: the hydrogen adsorbed will be replaced by the magnesium (Mg) and sodium (Na) present in the sea water.

Geographical Distribution

Acid sulfate soils are widespread around coastal regions, and are also locally associated with freshwater wetlands and saline sulfate-rich groundwater in some agricultural areas. In Australia, coastal acid sulfate soils occupy an estimated 80,000 km^2, underlying coastal estuaries and floodplains near where the majority of the Australian population lives. Acid sulfate soil disturbance is often associated with dredging, excavation dewatering activities during canal, housing and marina developments.

Acid sulfate soils which have not been disturbed are known as potential acid sulfate soils (PASS); acid sulfate soils which have been disturbed are known as actual acid sulfate soils (AASS).

Impacts of Acid Sulfate Soil

Disturbing potential acid sulfate soils can have a destructive effect on plant and fish life, and on coastal ecosystems. Flushing of acidic leachate to groundwater and surface waters can cause a number of impacts, including:

- Ecological damage to aquatic and riparian ecosystems through fish kills, increased fish disease outbreaks, dominance of acid-tolerant species, precipitation of iron, etc.
- Effects on estuarine fisheries and aquaculture projects (increased disease, loss of spawning area, etc).
- Contamination of groundwater with arsenic, aluminium and other heavy metals.
- Reduction in agricultural productivity through metal contamination of soils (predominantly by aluminium).
- Damage to infrastructure through the corrosion of concrete and steel pipes, bridges and other sub-surface assets.

Agricultural Impacts

Potentially acid sulfate soils (also called cat-clays) are often not cultivated or, if they are, planted under rice, so that the soil can be kept wet preventing oxi-dation. Subsurface drainage of these soils is normally not advisable.

When cultivated, acid sulfate soils cannot be kept wet continuously because of climatic dry spells and shortages of irrigation water, sur-face drainage may help to remove the acidic and toxic chemi-cals (formed in the dry spells) during rainy periods. In the long run surface drainage can help to reclaim acid sulfate soils. The indigenous population of Guinea Bissau has thus managed to develop the soils, but it has taken them many years of careful management and toil.

In an article on cautious land drainage the author describes the successful application of subsurface drainage in acid sulfate soils in coastal polders of Kerala state, India.

Also in the Sunderbans, West Bengal, India, acid sulfate soils have been taken in agricultural use.

A study in South Kalimantan, Indonesia, in a perhumid climate, has shown that the acid sulfate soils with a widely spaced subsurface drainage system have yielded promising results for the cultivation of upland (*sic*!) rice, pea nut and soy bean. The local population, of old, had already settled in this area and were able to produce a variety of crops (including tree fruits), using hand-dug drains running from the river into the land until reaching the back swamps. The crop yields were modest, but provided enough income to make a decent living.

Reclaimed cat-clays have a well developed soil structure, they are well permeable, but infertile due to the leaching that has occurred.

In the second half of the 20th century, in many parts of the world, waterlogged and potentially acid sulfate soils have been drained aggressively to make them productive for agriculture. The results were disastrous. The soils are unproductive, the lands look barren and the water is very clear, devoid of silt and life. The soils can be colourful, though.

Cation Exchange Capacity

In soil science, cation exchange capacity (CEC) is the capacity of a soil for ion exchange of positively charged ions between the soil and the soil solution. (A positively-charged ion, which has fewer electrons than protons, is known as a cation.) Cation exchange capacity is used as a measure of fertility, nutrient retention capacity, and the capacity to protect groundwater from cation contamination.

The quantity of positively charged ions (cations) that a clay mineral or similar material can accommodate on its negatively charged surface is expressed as milli-ion equivalent per 100 g, or more commonly as milliequivalent (meq) per 100 g. Clays are aluminosilicates in which some of the aluminium and silicon ions have been replaced by elements with different valence, or charge. For example, aluminium (Al_3^+) may be replaced by iron (Fe_2^+) or magnesium (Mg_2^+), leading to a net negative charge. This charge attracts cations when the clay is immersed in an electrolyte such as salty water and causes an electrical double layer. The cation-exchange capacity is often expressed in terms of its contribution per unit pore volume, Qv.

Base Saturation

Closely related to cation exchange capacity is the base saturation, which is the fraction of exchangeable cations that are base cations (Ca, Mg, K and Na). The higher the amount of exchangeable base cations, the more acidity can be neutralised in the short time perspective. Thus, a site with high cation exchange capacity takes longer time to acidify (as well as to recover from an acidified status) than a site with a low cation exchange capacity (assuming similar base saturations).

Laboratory Determination

There are two standardised International Soil Reference and Information Centre methods for determining CEC:

— extraction with ammonium acetate; and

— the silver-thiourea method (one-step centrifugal extraction).

There exist slightly conflicting ideas on which mechanisms to include in the term, "cation exchange", in soil chemistry. From a theoretical point of view, one should distinguish cation exchange from ligand exchange, and exchange of diffuse layer adsorbed cations. On the other hand, from a practical point of view, e.g. in forest and agricultural management, what is important is the soils' ability to replace one cation with another rather than the exact mechanism by which this replacement occurs. What is included in the term, "cation exchange", in soil science thus varies with the scientific context.

ORGANIC HORTICULTURE

Organic horticulture is the science and art of growing fruits, vegetables, flowers, or ornamental plants by following the essential principles of organic agriculture in soil building and conservation, pest management, and heritage-species preservation.

The Latin words 'hortus' (garden plant) and 'cultura' (culture) together form horticulture, classically defined as the culture or growing of garden plants. Horticulture is also sometimes defined simply as "agriculture minus the plough (or plow)." Instead of the plough, horticulture makes use of human labour and gardener's cultivation tools, or of small machine tools like rotary tillers.

General

Mulches, cover crops, compost, manures, and ground-rock mineral supplements are soil-building mainstays. Through care and good soil condition, it is hoped that insect, fungal,or other problems that sometimes plague plants can be avoided. However, pheromone traps, insecticidal soap sprays, and other pest-control methods available to organic farmers are also sometimes utilized by organic horticulturists.

Horticulture involves five areas of study. These areas are floriculture (includes production and marketing of floral crops), landscape horticulture (includes production, marketing and maintenance of landscape plants), olericulture (includes production and marketing of vegetables), pomology (includes production and marketing of fruits), and postharvest physiology (involves maintaining quality and preventing spoilage of horticultural crops). All of these can be, and sometimes are, pursued according to the principles of organic cultivation.

Organic horticulture (or organic gardening) is based on knowledge and techniques gathered over thousands of years. In general terms, organic horticulture involves natural processes, often taking place over extended periods of time, and a holistic approach - while chemical-based horticulture focuses on immediate, isolated effects and reductionist strategies.

Organic Gardening Systems

There are a number of formal organic gardening and farming systems that prescribe specific techniques. They tend to be more specific than, and fit within, general organic standards. Biodynamic farming is an approach based on the esoteric teachings of Rudolf Steiner. The Japanese farmer and writer Masanobu Fukuoka invented a no-till system for small-scale grain production that he called Natural Farming. French intensive and biointensive methods and SPIN Farming (Small Plot INtensive) are all small scale gardening techniques.

A garden is more than just a means of providing food, it is a model of what is possible in a community - everyone could have a garden of some kind (container, growing box, raised bed) and produce healthy, nutritious organic food - promoting a more sustainable way of living that would encourage their local economy - a farmers market, a place to pass on gardening experience, and a sharing of bounty. A simple 4' × 8' (32 square feet) raised bed garden based on the principles of bio-intensive planting and square foot gardening uses fewer nutrients and less water, and could keep a family, or community, supplied with an abundance of healthy, nutritious organic greens, while promoting a more sustainable way of living.

Pest Control Approaches

Differing approaches to pest control are equally notable. In chemical horticulture, a specific insecticide may be applied to quickly kill off a particular insect pest. Chemical controls can dramatically reduce pest populations in the short term, yet by unavoidably killing (or starving) natural predator insects and animals, cause an increase in the pest population in the long term. Repeated use of insecticides and herbicides and other pesticides also encourages rapid natural selection of resistant insects, plants and other organisms, necessitating increased use, or requiring new, more powerful controls.

Organic Pest Control Techniques

In contrast, organic horticulture tends to tolerate some pest populations while taking the long view. Organic pest control requires a thorough understanding of pest life cycles and interactions, and involves the cumulative effect of many techniques, including:

- Allowing for an acceptable level of pest damage;
- Encouraging predatory beneficial insects to flourish and eat pests;
- Encouraging beneficial microorganisms;
- Careful plant selection, choosing disease-resistant varieties;
- Planting companion crops that discourage or divert pests;
- Using row covers to protect crop plants during pest migration periods;
- Rotating crops to different locations from year to year to interrupt pest reproduction cycles; and
- Using insect traps to monitor and control insect populations.

Each of these techniques also provides other benefits, such as soil protection and improvement, fertilization, pollination, water conservation and season extension. These benefits are both complementary and cumulative in overall effect on site health. Organic pest control and biological pest control can be used as part of integrated pest management (IPM). However, IPM also allows the use of chemical pesticides that are not part of organic or biological techniques.

CHAPTER–3

Clay Minerals

INTRODUCTION

Clay minerals are hydrous aluminium phyllosilicates, sometimes with variable amounts of iron, magnesium, alkali metals, alkaline earths and other cations. Clays have structures similar to the micas and therefore form flat hexagonal sheets. Clay minerals are common weathering products (including weathering of feldspar) and low temperature hydrothermal alteration products.

Clay minerals are very common in fine grained sedimentary rocks such as shale, mudstone and siltstone and in fine grained metamorphic slate and phyllite. Clays are ultra fine grained (normally considered to be less than 2 microns in size on standard particle size classifications) and so require special analytical techniques.

Standards include x-ray diffraction, electron diffraction methods, various spectrscopic methods such as Mossbauer spectroscopy, infrared spectroscopy, and EDS or energy dispersive spectroscopy. These methods should always augment standard polarized light microscopy, a technique which is sometimes overlooked but often where fundamental occurrences or petrologic relationships are established.

Clays are commonly referred to as 1:1 or 2:1. Clays are fundamentally built of tetrahedral sheets and octahedral sheets, as described in the Structure section in the following pages. A 1:1 clay would consist of one tetrahedral sheet and one octahedral sheet, and examples would be kaolinite and serpentine. A 2:1 clay consists of an octahedral sheet sandwiched between two tetrahedral sheets, and examples are illite, smectite, attapulgite, and chlorite (although chlorite has an external octahedral sheet often referred to as "brucite").

Clay minerals include the following groups:

— Kaolin group which includes the minerals kaolinite, dickite, halloysite and nacrite.

— Some sources include the serpentine group due to structural similarities (Bailey 1980).

— Smectite group which includes dioctahedral smectites such as montmorillonite and nontronite and trioctahedral smectites for example saponite.

— Illite group which includes the clay-micas. Illite is the only common mineral.

— Chlorite group includes a wide variety of similar minerals with considerable chemical variation.

— Other 2 to 1 clay types exist such as sepiolite or attapulgite, clays with long water channels internal to their structure.

Mixed layer clay variations exist for most of the above groups. Ordering is described as random or regular ordering, and is further described by the term Reicheweite, which is German for ordering. Literature articles will refer to a R1 ordered illite-smectite, for example. This type would be ordered in an ISISIS fashion. R0 on the other hand describes random ordering, and other advanced ordering types are also found (R3, etc). Mixed layer clay minerals which are perfect R1 types often get their own names. R1 ordered chlorite-smectite is known as corrensite, R1 illite-smectite is rectorite.

History

Knowledge of the nature of clay became better understood in the 1930s with advancements in x-ray diffraction technology necessary to analyze the molecular nature of clay particles.

Standardization in terminology arose during this period as well with special attention given to similar words that resulted in confusion such as sheet and plane.

The Clay Minerals Society, a scientific organisation dedicated to the investigation of clays and clay-sized particles, was chartered in 1963. This society, sometimes referred to as the CMS, has a strong global membership and many web resources. The journal of the CMS is called Clays and Clay Minerals and publishes 6 issues per year dedicated to the study of clays, their intrinsic properties, clay diagenesis, mineralogy, and geologic occurrences.

Structure

Like all phyllosilicates, clay minerals are characterised by two-dimensional sheets of corner sharing SiO_4 and AlO_4 tetrahedra. These tetrahedral sheets have the chemical composition $(Al,Si)_3O_4$, and each tetrahedron shares 3 of its vertex oxygen atoms with other tetrahedra forming a hexagonal array in two-dimensions. The fourth vertex is not shared with another tetrahedron and all of the tetrahedra "point" in the same direction (i.e. all of the unshared vertices are on the same side of the sheet).

In clays the tetrahedral sheets are always bonded to octahedral sheets formed from small cations, such as aluminium or magnesium, coordinated by six oxygen atoms. The unshared vertex from the tetrahedral sheet also form part of one side of the octahedral sheet but an additional oxygen atom is located above the gap in the tetrahedral sheet at the center of the six tetrahedra. This oxygen atom is bonded to a hydrogen atom forming an OH group in the clay structure. Clays can be categorised depending on the way that tetrahedral and octahedral sheets are packaged into layers. If there is only one tetrahedral and one octahedral group in each layer the clay is known as a 1:1 clay. The alternative, known as a 2:1 clay, has two tetrahedral sheets with the unshared vertex of each sheet pointing towards each other and forming each side of the octahedral sheet.

Bonding between the tetrahedral and octahedral sheets requires that the tetrahedral sheet becomes corrogated or twisted, causing ditrigonal distortion to the hexagonal array, and the octahedral sheet is flattened. This minimizes the overall bond-valence distortions of the crystallite.

Depending on the composition of the tetrahedral and octahedral heets, the layer will have no charge, or will have a net negative charge. If the layers are charged this charge is balanced by interlayer cations such as Na^+ or K^+. In each case the interlayer can also contain water. The crystal structure is formed from a stack of layers interspaced with the interlayers.

CLAY ANIMATION

Clay animation is one of many forms of stop motion animation. Each animated piece, either character or background, is "deformable"—made of a malleable substance, usually Plasticine clay. The portmanteau term "Claymation" is a registered trademark in the United States, registered by Will Vinton in 1978 to describe his clay animated films. While the word is not considered a genericized trademark, it has become a trademark which is often used generically in the US to refer to any animation using plasticene or similar substance.

All traditional animation is produced in a similar fashion, whether done through cel animation or stop-motion. Each frame, or still picture, is recorded on film or digital media and then played back in rapid succession. When played back at a frame rate greater than 10-12 frames per second, a fairly convincing illusion of continuous motion is achieved. While the play-back feature creating an illusion is true of all moving image (from zoetrope, to films to videogames), the techniques involved in creating CGI are generally removed from a frame-by-frame process.

Technique

In clay animation, which is one of the many forms of stop motion animation, each object is sculpted in clay or a similarly pliable material such as Plasticine, usually around a wire skeleton called an armature. As in other forms of object animation, the object is arranged on the set (background), a film frame is taken and the object or character is then moved slightly by hand. Another frame is taken and the object moved slightly again. This cycle is repeated until the animator has achieved the desired amount of film. The human mind processes the series of slightly changing, rapidly playing images as motion, hence making it appear that the object is moving by itself. To achieve the best results, a consistent shooting environment is needed to maintain the illusion of continuity. This means paying special attention to maintaining consistent lighting and object placement and working in a calm environment.

Production

Producing a stop motion animation using clay is extremely laborious. Normal film runs at 24 frames per second (frame/s). With the standard practice of "doubles" or "twos" (double-framing—exposing 2 frames for each shot), 12 changes are usually made for one second of film movement. For a 30-minute movie, there would be approximately 21,600 stops to change the figures for the frames. For a full length (90 min) movie, there would be approximately 64,800 stops and possibly far more if parts were shot with "singles" or "ones" (one frame exposed for each shot). Great care must be taken to ensure the object is not altered by accident, by even slight smudges, dirt, hair, or even dust. For feature-length productions, the use of clay has generally been supplanted by rubber silicone and resin-cast components. One foam-rubber process has been coined as Foamation by Will Vinton. However, clay remains a viable animation material where a particular aesthetic is desired.

A sub-variation of clay animation can be informally called "clay melting". Any kind of heat source can be applied on or near (or below) clay to cause it to melt while an animation camera on a time-lapse setting slowly films the process. An example of this can be seen in Vinton's early short clay-animated film, Closed Mondays, (co-produced by animator Bob Gardiner) at the end of the computer sequence. A similar technique was used in the climax scene of Raiders of the Lost Ark to "melt" the faces of the antagonists.

Types

Clay animation can take several forms:

"Freeform" clay animation is an informal term where the shape of the clay changes radically as the animation progresses. Or clay can take the form of "character" clay animation where the clay maintains a recognizable character throughout a shot.

One variation of clay animation is strata-cut animation in which a long bread-like loaf of clay, internally packed tight and loaded with varying imagery, is sliced into thin sheets, with the camera taking a frame of the end of the loaf for each cut, eventually revealing the movement of the internal images within. Pioneered in both clay and blocks of wax by German animator Oskar Fischinger during the 1920s and 30s, the technique was revivied and highly refined in the mid-90s by David Daniels, an associate of Will Vinton, in his 16-minute short film Buzz Box.

Another clay animation technique, and blurring the distinction between stop motion and traditional flat animation, is called clay painting (which is also a variation of the direct manipulation animation process) where clay is placed on a flat surface and moved like wet oil paints as on a traditional artistic canvas to produce any style of images, but with a clay 'look' to them.

Pioneering this technique was one-time Vinton animator Joan Gratz, first in her Oscar-nominated film The Creation (1980) and then in her Oscar-winning Mona Lisa Descending a Staircase filmed in 1992.

Already 1972 animated André Roche in the Cineplast Films Studio of Marc Chinoy in Munich (Germany) several films for a serie named Kli-Kla-Klawitter for the Second German TV-Channel ZDF, for a German language teaching serie for foreign children and another one for a traffic education serie (Herr Daniel paßt auf = Mr. Daniel cares of).

A variation of this technique was developed by another Vinton animator, Craig Bartlett, for his series of "Arnold" short films, also made during the 90s, in which he not only used clay painting, but sometimes built up clay images that rose off the plane of the flat support platform, toward the camera lens, to give a more 3-D stop-motion look to his films.

Some of the best-known clay-animated works include the Gumby series of television show segments created by Art Clokey, and the TV commercial made for the California Raisin Advisory Board by Vinton's studio. Clay animation has also been used in Academy-Award-winning short films such as Closed Mondays (Will Vinton and Bob Gardiner, 1974), The Sand Castle (1977), Creature Comforts (Aardman, 1989), and all three Wallace & Gromit short films, created by Nick Park of Aardman Animation. Aardman also created The Presentators, a series of one-minute clay-animation short films aired on Nicktoons. Some clay animations appear online, on such sites as Newgrounds.

Several computer games have also been produced using clay animation, including *The Neverhood, Dark Oberon, Clay Fighter, Platypus, Primal Rage* and the *Cletus Clay*. Television commercials have also utilized the clay animation, such as the *Chevron Cars* ads, produced by Aardman Studios. Besides commercials, clay animation has also been popularized in recent years by children's shows such as *Bob the Builder* and *The Koala Brothers*, as well as adult-oriented shows on Cartoon Network's *Adult Swim* lineup, including *Robot Chicken* (which uses clay animation and action figures as stop-motion puppets in conjunction) and Moral Orel. Many independent young film makers have used clay animation features for internet viewing.

CERAMIC

Ceramic, which is derived from the Greek word 'keramikos', covers inorganic and non-metallic materials which are formed by the action of heat. Up until the 1950s or so, the most important of these were the traditional clays, made into pottery, bricks, tiles and the like, along with cements and glass. Clay-based ceramics are described in the article on pottery. A composite material of ceramic and metal is known as cermet. The word ceramic can be an adjective, and can also be used as a noun to refer to a ceramic material, or a product of ceramic manufacture. Ceramics may also be used as a singular noun referring to the art of making things out of ceramic materials. The technology of manufacturing and usage of ceramic materials is part of the field of ceramic engineering.

Many ceramic materials are hard, porous, and brittle. The study and development of ceramics includes methods to mitigate problems associated with these characteristics, and to accentuate the strengths of the materials as well as to investigate novel applications.

The American Society for Testing and Materials (ASTM) defines a ceramic article as "an article having a glazed or unglazed body of crystalline or partly crystalline structure, or of glass, which body is produced from essentially inorganic, non-metallic substances and either is formed from a molten mass which solidifies on cooling, or is formed and simultaneously or subsequently matured by the action of the heat."

Types of Ceramic Materials

For convenience ceramic products are usually divided into four sectors, and these are shown below with some examples:

— Structural, including bricks, pipes, floor and roof tiles.

— Refractories, such as kiln linings, gas fire radiants, steel and glass making crucibles.

— Whitewares, including tableware, wall tiles, decorative art objects and sanitary ware.

Technical, is also known as Engineering, Advanced, Special, and in Japan, Fine Ceramics. Such items include tiles used in the Space Shuttle programme, gas burner nozzles, ballistic protection, nuclear fuel uranium oxide pellets, bio-medical implants, jet engine turbine blades, and missile nose cones. Frequently the raw materials do not include clays.

EXAMPLES OF WHITEWARE CERAMICS

Bone China

— Earthenware, which is often made from clay, quartz and feldspar.

— Porcelain, which are often made from kaolin

— Stoneware

Classification of Technical Ceramics

Technical ceramics can also be classified into three distinct material categories:

— Oxides: Alumina, zirconia.

— Non-oxides: Carbides, borides, nitrides, silicides.

— Composites: Particulate reinforced, combinations of oxides and non-oxides.

— Each one of these classes can develop unique material properties.

Examples of Technical Ceramics

— Barium titanate (often mixed with strontium titanate) displays ferroelectricity, meaning that its mechanical, electrical, and thermal responses are coupled to one another and also history-dependent. It is widely used in electromechanical transducers, ceramic capacitors, and data storage elements. Grain boundary conditions can create PTC effects in heating elements.

— Bismuth strontium calcium copper oxide, a high-temperature superconductor.

— Boron nitride is structurally isoelectronic to carbon and takes on similar physical forms: a graphite-like one used as a lubricant, and a diamond-like one used as an abrasive.

— Ferrite (Fe_3O_4), which is ferrimagnetic and is used in the magnetic cores of electrical transformers and magnetic core memory.

— Lead zirconate titanate is another ferroelectric material.

— Magnesium diboride (MgB_2), which is an unconventional superconductor.

— Sialons/Silicon Aluminium Oxynitrides, high strength, high thermal shock/chemical/wear resistance, low density ceramics used in non-ferrous molten metal handling, weld pins and the chemical industry.

— Silicon carbide (SiC), which is used as a susceptor in microwave furnaces, a commonly used abrasive, and as a refractory material.

— Silicon nitride (Si_3N_4), which is used as an abrasive powder.

— Steatite (magnesium silicates) is used as an electrical insulator.

— Titanium Carbide Used in space shuttle re-entry shields and scratchproof watches.

— Uranium oxide (UO_2), used as fuel in nuclear reactors.

— Yttrium barium copper oxide (YBa2Cu3O7-x), another high temperature superconductor.

— Zinc oxide (ZnO), which is a semiconductor, and used in the construction of varistors.

— Zirconium dioxide (zirconia), which in pure form undergoes many phase changes between room temperature and practical sintering temperatures, can be chemically "stabilized" in several different forms. Its high oxygen ion conductivity recommends it for use in fuel cells. In another variant, metastable structures can impart transformation toughening for mechanical applications; most ceramic knife blades are made of this material.

Properties of Ceramics

Mechanical Properties

Ceramic materials are usually ionic or covalent bonded materials, and can be crystalline or amorphous. A material held together by either type of bond will tend to fracture before any plastic deformation takes place, which results in poor toughness in these materials. Additionally, because these materials tend to be porous, the pores and other microscopic imperfections act as stress concentrators, decreasing the toughness further, and reducing the tensile strength. These combine to give catastrophic failures, as opposed to the normally much more gentle failure modes of metals.

These materials do show plastic deformation. However, due to the rigid structure of the crystalline materials, there are very few available slip systems for dislocations to move, and so they deform very slowly. With the non-crystalline (glassy) materials, viscous flow is the dominant source of plastic deformation, and is also very slow. It is therefore neglected in many applications of ceramic materials.

Electrical Properties

Semiconductors

There are a number of ceramics that are semiconductors. Most of these are transition metal oxides that are II-VI semiconductors, such as zinc oxide.

While there is talk of making blue LEDs from zinc oxide, ceramicists are most interested in the electrical properties that show grain boundary effects.

One of the most widely used of these is the varistor. These are devices that exhibit the property that resistance drops sharply at a certain threshold voltage. Once the voltage across the device reaches the threshold, there is a breakdown of the electrical structure in the vicinity of the grain boundaries, which results in its electrical resistance dropping from several megohms down to a few hundred ohms. The major advantage of these is that they can dissipate a lot of energy, and they self reset — after the voltage across the device drops below the threshold, its resistance returns to being high.

This makes them ideal for surge-protection applications. As there is control over the threshold voltage and energy tolerance, they find use in all sorts of applications. The best demonstration of their ability can be found in electrical substations, where they are employed to protect the infrastructure from lightning strikes. They have rapid response, are low maintenance, and do not appreciably degrade from use, making them virtually ideal devices for this application.

Semiconducting ceramics are also employed as gas sensors. When various gases are passed over a polycrystalline ceramic, its electrical resistance changes. With tuning to the possible gas mixtures, very inexpensive devices can be produced.

Superconductivity

Under some conditions, such as extremely low temperature, some ceramics exhibit high temperature superconductivity. The exact reason for this is not known, but there are two major families of superconducting ceramics.

Ferroelectricity and Supersets

Piezoelectricity, a link between electrical and mechanical response, is exhibited by a large number of ceramic materials, including the quartz used to measure time in watches and other electronics. Such devices use both properties of piezoelectrics, using electricity to produce a mechanical motion (powering the device) and then using this mechanical motion to produce electricity (generating a signal). The unit of time measured is the natural interval required for electricity to be converted into mechanical energy and back again.

The piezoelectric effect is generally stronger in materials that also exhibit pyroelectricity, and all pyroelectric materials are also piezoelectric. These materials can be used to inter convert between thermal, mechanical, and/or electrical energy; for instance, after synthesis in a furnace, a pyroelectric crystal allowed to cool under no applied stress generally builds up a static charge of thousands of volts. Such materials are used in motion sensors, where the tiny rise in temperature from a warm body entering the room is enough to produce a measurable voltage in the crystal.

In turn, pyroelectricity is seen most strongly in materials which also display the ferroelectric effect, in which a stable electric dipole can be oriented or reversed by applying an electrostatic field. Pyroelectricity is also a necessary consequence of ferroelectricity. This can be used to store information in ferroelectric capacitors, elements of ferroelectric RAM.

The most common such materials are lead zirconate titanate and barium titanate. Aside from the uses mentioned above, their strong piezoelectric response is exploited in the design of high-frequency loudspeakers, transducers for sonar, and actuators for atomic force and scanning tunneling microscopes.

POSITIVE THERMAL COEFFICIENT

Increases in temperature can cause grain boundaries to suddenly become insulating in some semiconducting ceramic materials, mostly mixtures of heavy metal titanates. The critical transition temperature can be adjusted over a wide range by variations in chemistry. In such materials, current will pass through the material until joule heating brings it to the transition temperature, at which point the circuit will be broken and current flow will cease. Such ceramics are used as self-controlled heating elements in, for example, the rear-window defrost circuits of automobiles.

At the transition temperature, the material's dielectric response becomes theoretically infinite. While a lack of temperature control would rule out any practical use of the material near its critical temperature, the dielectric effect remains exceptionally strong even at much higher temperatures. Titanates with critical temperatures far below room temperature have become synonymous with "ceramic" in the context of ceramic capacitors for just this reason.

CLASSIFICATION OF CERAMICS

Non-crystalline Ceramics

Non-crystalline ceramics, being glasses, tend to be formed from melts. The glass is shaped when either fully molten, by casting, or when in a state of toffee-like viscosity, by methods such as blowing to a mold. If later heat-treatments cause this class to become partly crystalline, the resulting material is known as a glass-ceramic.

Crystalline Ceramics

Crystalline ceramic materials are not amenable to a great range of processing. Methods for dealing with them tend to fall into one of two categories - either make the ceramic in the desired shape, by reaction in situ, or by "forming" powders into the desired shape, and then sintering to form a solid body. Ceramic forming techniques include shaping by hand (sometimes including a rotation process called "throwing"), slip casting, tape casting (used for making very thin ceramic capacitors, etc.), injection molding, dry pressing, and other variations. A few methods use a hybrid between the two approaches.

In situ Manufacturing

The most common use of this method is in the production of cement and concrete. Here, the dehydrated powders are mixed with water. This starts hydration reactions, which result in long, interlocking crystals forming around the aggregates. Over time, these result in a solid ceramic.

The biggest problem with this method is that most reactions are so fast that good mixing is not possible, which tends to prevent large-scale construction. However, small-scale systems can be made by deposition techniques, where the various materials are introduced above a substrate, and react and form the ceramic on the substrate. This borrows techniques from the semi-conductor industry, such as chemical vapour deposition, and is very useful for coatings.

These tend to produce very dense ceramics, but do so slowly.

Sintering-based Methods

The principles of sintering-based methods is simple. Once a roughly held together object (called a "green body") is made, it is baked in a kiln, where diffusion processes cause the green body to shrink. The pores in the object close up, resulting in a denser, stronger product. The firing is done at a temperature below the melting point of the ceramic. There is virtually always some porosity left, but the real advantage of this method is that the green body can be produced in any way imaginable, and still be sintered. This makes it a very versatile route.

There are thousands of possible refinements of this process. Some of the most common involve pressing the green body to give the densification a head start and reduce the sintering time needed. Sometimes organic binders such as polyvinyl alcohol are added to hold the green body together; these burn out during the firing (at 200–350°C). Sometimes organic lubricants are added during pressing to increase densification. It is not uncommon to combine these, and add binders and lubricants to a powder, then press. (The formulation of these organic chemical additives is an art in itself. This is particularly important in the manufacture of high performance ceramics such as those used by the billions for electronics, in capacitors, inductors, sensors, etc.

A slurry can be used in place of a powder, and then cast into a desired shape, dried and then sintered. Indeed, traditional pottery is done with this type of method, using a plastic mixture worke with the hands.

If a mixture of different materials is used together in a ceramic, the sintering temperature is sometimes above the melting point of one minor component - a liquid phase sintering. This results in shorter sintering times compared to solid state sintering.

Other Applications of Ceramics

Ceramics are used in the manufacture of knives. The blade of the ceramic knife will stay sharp for much longer than that of a steel knife, although it is more brittle and can be snapped by dropping it on a hard surface.

Ceramics such as alumina and boron carbide have been used in ballistic armored vests to repel large-caliber rifle fire. Such plates are known commonly as small-arms protective inserts (SAPI). Similar material is used to protect cockpits of some military airplanes, because of the low weight of the material.

Ceramic balls can be used to replace steel in ball bearings. Their higher hardness means that they are much less susceptible to wear and can offer more than triple lifetimes. They also deform less under load meaning they have less contact with the bearing retainer walls and can roll faster. In very high speed applications, heat from friction during rolling can cause problems for metal bearings; problems which are reduced by the use of ceramics. Ceramics are also more chemically resistant and can be used in wet environments where steel bearings would rust. The major drawback to using ceramics is a significantly higher cost. In many cases their electrically insulating properties may also be valuable in bearings.

In the early 1980s, Toyota researched production of an adiabatic ceramic engine which can run at a temperature of over 6000 °F (3300 °C). Ceramic engines do not require a cooling system and hence allow a major weight reduction and therefore greater fuel efficiency. Fuel efficiency of the engine is also higher at high temperature, as shown by Carnot's theorem. In a conventional metallic engine, much of the energy released from the fuel must be dissipated as waste heat in order to prevent a meltdown of the metallic parts. Despite all of these desirable properties, such engines are not in production because the manufacturing of ceramic parts in the requisite precision and durability is difficult. Imperfection in the ceramic leads to cracks, which can lead to potentially dangerous equipment failure. Such engines are possible in laboratory settings, but mass-production is not feasible with current technology.

Work is being done in developing ceramic parts for gas turbine engines. Currently, even blades made of advanced metal alloys used in the engines' hot section require cooling and careful limiting of operating temperatures. Turbine engines made with ceramics could operate more efficiently, giving aircraft greater range and payload for a set amount of fuel.

Recently, there have been advances in ceramics which include bio-ceramics, such as dental implants and synthetic bones. Hydroxyapatite, the natural mineral component of bone, has been made synthetically from a number of biological and chemical sources and can be formed into ceramic materials. Orthopedic implants made from these materials bond readily to bone and other tissues in the body without rejection or inflammatory reactions. Because of this, they are of great interest for gene delivery and tissue engineering scaffolds. Most hydroxy apatite ceramics are very porous and lack mechanical strength and are used to coat metal orthopedic devices to aid in forming a bond to bone or as bone fillers. They are also used as fillers for orthopedic plastic screws to aid in reducing the inflammation and increase absorption of these plastic materials. Work is being done to make strong, fully dense nano crystalline hydroxapatite ceramic materials for orthopedic weight bearing devices, replacing foreign metal and plastic orthopedic materials with a synthetic, but naturally occurring, bone mineral. Ultimately these ceramic materials may be used as bone replacements or with the incorporation of protein collagens, synthetic bones.

High-tech ceramic is used in watchmaking for producing watch cases. The material is valued by watchmakers for its light weight, scratch-resistance, durability and smooth touch. IWC is one of the brands that initiated the use of ceramic in watchmaking. The case of the IWC 2007 Top Gun edition of the Pilot's Watch Double chronograph is crafted in high-tech black ceramic.

CHAPTER–4

Adsorption

INTRODUCTION

Adsorption is a process that occurs when a gas or liquid solute accumulates on the surface of a solid or a liquid (adsorbent), forming a film of molecules or atoms (the adsorbate). It is different from absorption, in which a substance diffuses into a liquid or solid to form a solution. The term sorption encompasses both processes, while desorption is the reverse process.

Adsorption is present in many natural physical, biological, and chemical systems, and is widely used in industrial applications such as activated charcoal, synthetic resins, and water purification. Adsorption, ion exchange, and chromatography are sorption processes in which certain adsorbates are selectively transferred from the fluid phase to the surface of insoluble, rigid particles suspended in a vessel or packed in a column.

Similar to surface tension, adsorption is a consequence of surface energy. In a bulk material, all the bonding requirements (be they ionic, covalent, or metallic) of the constituent atoms of the material are filled by other atoms in the material. However, atoms on the surface of the adsorbent are not wholly surrounded by other adsorbent atoms and therefore can attract adsorbates. The exact nature of the bonding depends on the details of the species involved, but the adsorption process is generally classified as physisorption (characteristic of weak van der Waals forces) or chemisorption (characteristic of covalent bonding).

ISOTHERMS

Adsorption is usually described through isotherms, that is, the amount of adsorbate on the adsorbent as a function of its pressure (if gas) or concentration (if liquid) at constant temperature. The quantity adsorbed is nearly always normalized by the mass of the adsorbent to allow comparison of different materials.

The first mathematical fit to an isotherm was published by Freundlich and Küster (1894) and is a purely empirical formula for gaseous adsorbates,

$$\frac{x}{m} = kP^{\frac{1}{n}}$$

where x is the quantity adsorbed, m is the mass of the adsorbent, P is the pressure of adsorbate and k and n are empirical constants for each adsorbent-adsorbate pair at a given temperature. The function has an asymptotic maximum as pressure increases without bound. As the temperature increases, the constants k and n change to reflect the empirical observation that the quantity adsorbed rises more slowly and higher pressures are required to saturate the surface.

Langmuir

In 1916, Irving Langmuir published a new model isotherm for gases adsorbed on solids, which retained his name. It is a semi-empirical isotherm derived from a proposed kinetic mechanism. It is based on four assumptions:

1. The surface of the adsorbent is uniform, that is, all the adsorption sites are equivalent.
2. Adsorbed molecules do not interact.
3. All adsorption occurs through the same mechanism.
4. At the maximum adsorption, only a monolayer is formed: molecules of adsorbate do not deposit on other, already adsorbed, molecules of adsorbate, only on the free surface of the adsorbent.

These four assumptions are seldom all true: there are always imperfections on the surface, adsorbed molecules are not necessarily inert, and the mechanism is clearly not the same for the very first molecules to adsorb as for the last. The fourth condition is the most troublesome, as frequently more molecules will adsorb on the monolayer; this problem is addressed by the BET isotherm for relatively flat (non-microporous) surfaces. The Langmuir isotherm is nonetheless the first choice for most models of adsorption, and has many applications in surface kinetics (usually called Langmuir-Hinshelwood kinetics) and thermodynamics.

Langmuir suggested that adsorption takes place through this mechanism:

$$A_g + S = AS$$

where A is a gas molecule and S is an adsorption site. The direct and inverse rate constants are k and $k{-1}$. If we define surface coverage, θ, as the fraction of the adsorption sites occupied, in the equilibrium we have

$$K = \frac{k}{k_{-1}} = \frac{\theta}{(1-\theta)P}$$

$$\theta = \frac{KP}{1+KP}$$

where P is the partial pressure (gas) or the molar concentration of the solution (gas). For very low pressures $\theta \approx KP$ and $\theta \approx 1$ for high pressures.

θ is difficult to measure experimentally; usually, the adsorbate is a gas and the quantity adsorbed is given in moles, grams, or gas volumes at standard temperature and pressure (STP) per gram of adsorbent. If we call vmon the STP volume of adsorbate required to form a monolayer on the adsorbent (per gram of adsorbent), $\theta = \frac{\upsilon}{\upsilon_{mon}}$ and we obtain an expression for a straight line:

$$\frac{1}{\upsilon}=\frac{1}{K\upsilon_{mon}}\frac{1}{P}+\frac{1}{\upsilon_{mon}}$$

Through its slope and y-intercept we can obtain v_{mon} and K, which are constants for each adsorbent/adsorbate pair at a given temperature. vmon is related to the number of adsorption sites through the ideal gas law. If we assume that the number of sites is just the whole area of the solid divided into the cross section of the adsorbate molecules, we can easily calculate the surface area of the adsorbent. The surface area of an adsorbent depends on its structure; the more pores it has, the greater the area, which has a big influence on reactions on surfaces.

If more than one gas adsorbs on the surface, we define θ_E as the fraction of empty sites and we have

$$\theta_E=\frac{1}{1+\sum_{i=1}^{n}K_iP_i}$$

and

$$\theta_j=\frac{K_jP_j}{1+\sum_{i=1}^{n}K_iP_i}$$

where i is each one of the gases that adsorb.

Often molecules do form multilayers, that is, some are adsorbed on already adsorbed molecules and the Langmuir isotherm is not valid. In 1938 Stephan Brunauer, Paul Emmett, and Edward Teller developed a model isotherm that takes that possibility into account. Their theory is called BET theory, after the initials in their last names. They modified Langmuir's mechanism as follows:

$A(g) + S \rightleftharpoons AS$

$A(g) + AS \rightleftharpoons A2S$

$A(g) + A2S \rightleftharpoons A3S$ and so on

The derivation of the formula is more complicated than Langmuir's). We obtain:

$$\frac{x}{V(1-x)} = \frac{1}{V_{mon}C} + \frac{x(c-1)}{V_{mon}C}$$

x is the pressure divided by the vapor pressure for the adsorbate at that temperature (usually denoted P/P_0), v is the STP volume of adsorbed adsorbate, v_{mon} is the STP volume of the amount of adsorbate required to form a monolayer and c is the equilibrium constant K we used in Langmuir isotherm multiplied by the vapor pressure of the adsorbate. The key assumption used in deriving the BET equation that the successive heats of adsorption for all layers except the first are equal to the heat of condensation of the adsorbate.

The Langmuir isotherm is usually better for chemisorption and the BET isotherm works better for physisorption for non-microporous surfaces.

ADSORPTION ENTHALPY

Adsorption constants are equilibrium constants, therefore they obey van 't Hoff's equation:

$$\left(\frac{\partial \ln K}{\partial \frac{1}{T}}\right)_{\theta} = -\frac{\Delta H}{R}$$

As can be seen in the formula, the variation of K must be isosteric, that is, at constant coverage. If we start from the BET isotherm and assume that the entropy change is the same for liquefaction and adsorption we obtain $\Delta H_{ads} = \Delta H_{liq} - RT\ln c$, that is to say, adsorption is more exothermic than liquefaction.

Adsorbents

Characteristics and General Requirements

Activated carbon is used as an adsorbentAdsorbents are used usually in the form of spherical pellets, rods, moldings, or monoliths with hydrodynamic diameters between 0.5 and 10 mm. They must have high abrasion resistance, high thermal stability and small pore diameters, which results in higher exposed surface area and hence high surface capacity for adsorption. The adsorbents must also have a distinct pore structure which enables fast transport of the gaseous vapours.

Most industrial adsorbents fall into one of three classes:

— Oxygen-containing compounds – Are typically hydrophilic and polar, including materials such as silica gel and zeolites.

— Carbon-based compounds – Are typically hydrophobic and non-polar, including materials such as activated carbon and graphite.

— Polymer-based compounds - Are polar or non-polar functional groups in a porous polymer matrix.

Silica gel

Silica gel is a chemically inert, nontoxic, polar and dimensionally stable (< 400 °C) amorphous form of SiO_2. It is prepared by the reaction between sodium silicate and sulfuric acid, which is followed by a series of after-treatment processes such as aging, pickling, etc. These after treatment methods results in various pore size distributions.

Silica is used for drying of process air (e.g. oxygen, natural gas) and adsorption of heavy (polar) hydrocarbons from natural gas.

ZEOLITES

Zeolites are natural or synthetic crystalline aluminosilicates which have a repeating pore network and release water at high temperature. Zeolites are polar in nature.

They are manufactured by hydrothermal synthesis of sodium aluminosilicate or another silica source in an autoclave followed by ion exchange with certain cations (Na^+, Li^+, Ca_2^+, K^+, NH_4^+). The channel diameter of zeolite cages usually ranges from 2 to 9 Å (200 to 900 pm). The ion exchange process is followed by drying of the crystals, which can be pelletized with a binder to form macroporous pellets.

Zeolites are applied in drying of process air, CO_2 removal from natural gas, CO_2 removal from reforming gas, air separation, catalytic cracking, and catalytic synthesis and reforming.

Non-polar (siliceous) zeolites are synthesized from aluminum-free silica sources or by dealumination of aluminum-containing zeolites. The dealumination process is done by treating the zeolite with steam at elevated temperatures, typically greater than 500 °C (1000 °F). This high temperature heat treatment breaks the aluminum-oxygen bonds and the aluminum atom is expelled from the zeolite framework.

ACTIVATED CARBON

Activated carbon is a highly porous, amorphous solid consisting of microcrystallites with a graphite lattice, usually prepared in small pellets or a powder. It is non-polar and cheap. One of its main drawbacks is that it is combustible.

Activated carbon nitrogen isotherm showing a marked microporous type I behaviour. Activated carbon can be manufactured from carbonaceous material, including coal (bituminous, subbituminous, and lignite), peat, wood, or nutshells (i.e., coconut). The manufacturing process consists of two phases, carbonization and activation. The carbonization process includes drying and then heating to separate by-products, including tars and other hydrocarbons, from the raw material, as well as to drive off any gases generated. The carbonization process is completed by heating the material at 400–600 °C in an oxygen-deficient atmosphere that cannot support combustion.

The carbonized particles are "activated" by exposing them to an oxidizing agent, usually steam or carbon dioxide at high temperature. This agent burns off the pore blocking structures created during the carbonization phase and so, they develop a porous, three-dimensional graphite lattice structure. The size of the pores developed during activation is a function of the time that they spend in this stage. Longer exposure times result in larger pore sizes. The most popular aqueous phase carbons are bituminous based because of their hardness, abrasion resistance, pore size distribution, and low cost, but their effectiveness needs to be tested in each application to determine the optimal product.

Activated carbon is used for adsorption of organic substances and non-polar adsorbates and it is also usually used for waste gas (and waste water) treatment. It is the most widely used adsorbent. Its usefulness derives mainly from its large micropore and mesopore volumes and the resulting high surface area.

Portal Site Mediated Adsorption

Portal site mediated adsorption is a model for site-selective activated gas adsorption in metallic catalytic systems which contain a variety of different adsorption sites. In such systems, low-coordination "edge and corner" defect-like sites can exhibit significantly lower adsorption enthalpies than high-coordination (basal plane) sites. As a result, these sites can serve as "portals" for very rapid adsorption to the rest of the surface. The phenomenon relies on the common "spillover" effect, where certain adsorbed species exhibit high mobility on some surfaces. The model explains seemingly inconsistent observations of gas adsorption thermodynamics and kinetics in catalytic systems where surfaces can exist in a range of coordination structures, and it has been successfully applied to bimetallic catalytic systems where synergistic activity is observed.

The original model was developed to describe hydrogen adsorption on silica-supported silver-ruthenium and copper-ruthenium bimetallic catalysts. The same group applied the model to CO hydrogenation (Fischer-Tropsch synthesis). Subsequently confirmed the same model on magnesia-supported cesium-ruthenium bimetallic catalysts.

Adsorption in Viruses

Adsorption is the first step in the viral infection cycle. The next steps are penetration, uncoating, synthesis (transcription if needed, and translation), and release. The virus replication cycle is similar, if not the same, for all types of viruses. Factors such as transcription may or may not be needed if the virus is able to integrate its genomic information in the cell's nucleus, or if the virus can replicate itself directly within the cell's cytoplasm.

DESORPTION

Desorption is a phenomenon whereby a substance is released from or through a surface. The process is the opposite of sorption (that is, adsorption and absorption). This occurs in a system being in the state of sorption equilibrium between bulk phase (fluid, i.e. gas or liquid solution) and an adsorbing surface (solid or boundary separating two fluids). When the concentration (or pressure) of substance in the bulk phase is lowered, some of the sorbed substance changes to the bulk state.

In chemistry, especially chromatography, desorption is the ability for a chemical to move with the mobile phase. The more a chemical desorbs, the less likely it will adsorb, thus instead of sticking to the stationary phase, the chemical moves up with the solvent front.

In chemical separation processes, stripping is also referred to as desorption as one component of a liquid stream moves by mass transfer into a vapor phase through the liquid-vapor interface.

After adsorption, the adsorbed chemical will remain on the substrate nearly indefinitely, provided the temperature remains low. However, as the temperature rises, so does the likelihood of desorption occurring. The general equation for the rate of desorption is:

$R = rNx$,

where r is the rate constant for desorption, N is the concentration of the adsorbed material, and x is the kinetic order of desorption.

Usually, the order of the desorption can be predicted by the number of elementary steps involved:

— Atomic or simple molecular desorption will typically be a first-order process (i.e. a simple molecule on the surface of the substrate desorbs into a gaseous form).

Recombinative molecular desorption will generally be a second-order process (i.e. two hydrogen atoms on the surface desorb and form a gaseous H_2 molecule).

The rate constant r may be expressed in the form:

$$r = A_e - {}^{E_a}\!/_{K_T}$$

where A is the "attempt frequency" (often the Greek letter υ), the chance of the adsorbed molecule overcoming its potential barrier to desorption, E_a is the activation energy of desorption, k is Boltzmann's constant, and T is the temperature.

CHAPTER–5

Soil Organic Matter

INTRODUCTION

Soil degradation has become a major concern in Canada. Erosion, salinization, acidification and loss of organic matter are the main forms of soil deterioration. This publication deals with the role of organic matter in soil productivity and the effects of various management practices on soil organic matter.

Soil organic matter consists of a variety of components. These include, in varying proportions and many Intermediate stages:

- raw plant residues and microorganisms (1 to 10 per cent)
- "active" organic traction (10 to 40 per cent)
- resistant or stable organic matter (40 to 60 per cent) also referred to as humus.

Raw plant residues, on the surface, help reduce surface wind speed and water runoff. Removal, incorporation or burning of residues predisposes the soil to serious erosion.

The "active" and some of the resistant soil organic components, together with microorganisms (especially fungi) are involved in binding small soil particles into larger aggregates. Aggregation is important for good soil structure, aeration, water infiltration and resistance to erosion and crusting.

The resistant or stable fraction of soil organic matter contributes mainly to *nutrient holding capacity* (cation exchange capacity) and *soil colour*. This fraction of organic matter decomposes very slowly and therefore has less influence on soil fertility than the "active" organic fraction.

Organic matter in soil serves several functions. From a practical agricultural standpoint, it is important for two main reasons. First as a "revolving nutrient bank account"; and second; as an agent to improve soil structure, maintain tilth, and minimize erosion.

As a *revolving nutrient bank account*, organic matter serves two main functions:

- Since soil organic matter is derived mainly from plant residues, it contains all of the essential plant nutrients. Accumulated organic matter, therefore, is a storehouse of plant nutrients. Upon decomposition, the nutrients are released in a plant-available form.
- The stable organic fraction (humus) adsorbs and holds nutrients in a plant available form.

Organic matter does not add any "new' plant nutrients but releases nutrients in a plant available form through the process of decomposition. In order to maintain this nutrient cycling system, the rate of addition from crop residues and manure must equal the rate of decomposition.

If the *rate of addition* is less than the *rate of decomposition*, soil organic matter will decline and, conversely if the rate of addition is greater than the rate of decomposition, soil organic matter will increase. The term steady state has been used to describe a condition where the rate of addition is equal to the rate of decomposition.

Fertilizer can contribute to the maintenance of this revolving nutrient bank account by increasing crop yields and consequently the amount of residues returned to the soil.

ORGANIC MATTER IN VIRGIN AND CULTIVATED SOILS

Soils in Alberta are divided into soil groups (zones) based on the amount of organic matter they contain. They occur in geographic zones from the southeast to the northwest and are identified as the Brown, Dark Brown, and Black Chernozemic (prairie) soils.

The Brown soils have the least amount of organic matter because of the relatively small inputs of plant residues contributed by the short grass prairie vegetation under which these soils developed. Black soils developed under cooler and wetter conditions which allowed for more grass growth and thus a greater accumulation of organic matter.

Further north and west, trees became the dominant vegetation. Soils influenced by forest vegetation for a moderate length of time constitute the Dark Gray or transitional soils. Where the forest cover was established for a longer period, Luvisolic (forest) soils developed. Organic (peat) soils. occur in low lying areas throughout the Black, Dark Gray and Gray soil zones. These soils are saturated with water for much or all of the year thereby reducing the rate of organic matter decomposition.

The amount of soil organic matter characteristic of virgin and cultivated soils in the various zones is shown in Table 5.1. Cultivation generally has resulted in a 30 to 50 per cent loss of organic matter.

Table 5.1: Organic matter in native and cultivated soils (per cent)

Soil zone	*Virgin*	*Cultivated*
Brown	3-4	2-3
Dark Brown	4-5	3-4
Black	6-10	4-6
Dark Gray	4-5	2-3
Gray	1-2	1-2

Before our soils were cultivated, they had achieved a "steady state". In most of our prairie soils, the increased rate of decomposition associated with cultivation, combined with the low rates of crop residue addition associated with crop-fallow rotations has caused a fairly rapid decline in soil organic matter.

The rate of decline decreases with time as the amount of total soil organic matter decreases and particularly as the "active" organic fraction is depleted.

Cultivation of soils that are naturally high in organic matter will usually result in a decrease of organic matter. In the case of Luvisolic soils, their poor physical properties and low fertility have encouraged the use of forages, fertilizers, manure and judicious tillage. Such management practices have resulted in an increase in soil organic matter on Luvisolic soils, whereas excessive tillage, fallowing and minimal fertilization have lead to further depletion of the soil organic matter.

EFFECTS OF ORGANIC MATTER DECLINE

As stated in the introduction, soil degradation is becoming a major concern in Canada. Loss of organic matter is often identified as one of the main factors contributing to declining soil productivity, but it is misleading to equate a loss in soil organic matter with a loss in soil productivity.

Soil organic matter contributes to soil productivity in several ways, but there is no direct quantitative relationship between soil productivity and total soil organic matter. In fact, it has been the decline in organic matter that has contributed to the productivity of the crop-fallow system.

This decline in organic matter has resulted in the release of large amounts of plant nutrients, particularly nitrogen. For example, a decrease in soil organic matter of 2 per cent releases about 2,400 lb/ac of nitrogen. If this decline occurred over a 60 year period, an average of 40 lb/ac/yr of plant-available nitrogen has come from the soil organic matter. We therefore view prairie soils which had relatively high levels of organic matter as being nitrogen fertile, but this fertility could only be attained under a management system that allowed for organic matter to decline. Frequent fallowing has been a major factor contributing to this decline.

Insofar as organic matter contributes to improved soil physical properties (e.g., tilth, aggregation, moisture holding capacity and resistance to erosion) increasing soil organic matter will generally result in increased soil productivity. But on many soils, suitable soil physical properties occur at relatively low levels of organic matter (2-4 per cent).

A level of organic matter higher than required to produce suitable physical properties is beneficial in that the soil has a greater buffering and nutrient holding capacity, but it does not contribute directly to soil productivity. If soils are managed so organic matter is not declining (steady-state), soils higher in organic matter (e.g., 8 per cent) are not inherently more productive or fertile than those that have less organic matter (e.g., 5 per cent).

To equate the ability to supply nutrients with total soil organic matter is not valid. The "active" fraction of organic matter is a more reliable indicator of soil fertility than is total soil organic matter. In cultivated soil, the "active" fraction is influence mainly by previous management.

Soil organic matter cannot be increased quickly even when management practices that conserve soil organic matter are adopted. The increased addition of organic matter associated with continuous cropping, and the production of higher crop yields, are accompanied by an increase in the rate of decomposition. Moreover, only a small fraction of crop residues added to soil remains as soil organic matter.

After an extended period of time, the return of all crop residues and the use of forages in rotations with cereals and oilseeds may significantly increase soil organic matter, particularly, the "active" fraction.

Managing Soil Organic Matter

There have been vast changes in the nature of agricultural production. In the past, farms were small, and much of what was produced was consumed on the farm. This system allowed for the limited removal of soil nutrients since there was an opportunity to return most of the nutrients back to the land.

The advent of the internal combustion engine, migration from rural to urban communities, increasing farm size and specialization in production have resulted in a system of production where there is greater removal of plant nutrients from the soil and less opportunity for nutrient cycling.

Maintenance of organic matter for the sake of maintenance alone is not a practical approach to farming. It is more realistic to use a management system that will give sustained profitable production.

The greatest source of soil organic matter is the residue contributed by current crops. Consequently, crop yield and type, method of handling residues and frequency of fallow are all important factors. Ultimately, soil organic matter must be maintained at a level necessary to maintain soil tilth. The effects of specific management practices are discussed below.

Summer-fallow

Summer-fallowing accelerates the loss of organic matter. Aeration of the soil associated with tillage, and the increase in soil temperature and moisture results in increased organic matter decomposition. Since little In the way of residues are added to the soil, a net loss of organic matter occurs. Research has shown that as the frequency of fallow increases, the amount of soil organic matter decreases (Fig. 5.1).

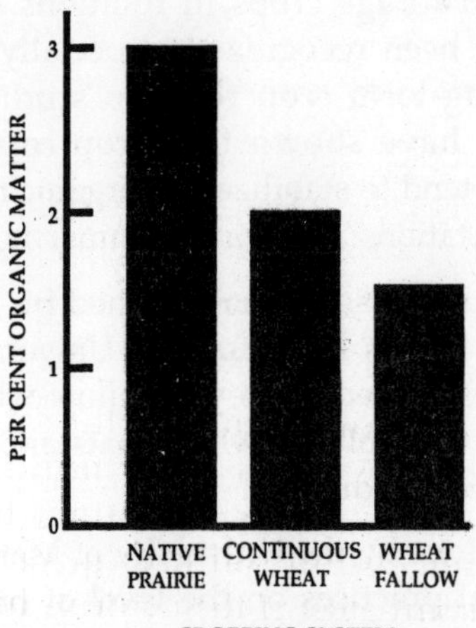

Fig. 5.1: Effect of frequency of fallow on per cent organic matter.

Summer-fallowing for moisture conservation may be a necessary practice in the Brown and Dark Brown soil zones. However, it must be questioned in the Black and the Gray soil zones. Periodic fallowing may be acceptable in the higher rainfall regions for control of persistent perennial weeds and volunteer grains in pedigreed seed production.

In the crop-fallow system common to the prairie region, the nitrogen removed has far exceeded that gained from crop residues, manure, legumes and fertilizer. The large reserves of nitrogen present in the organic matter of our prairie soils have been the major source of nitrogen in this cropping system. Continued reliance on soil organic matter reserves to supply the nitrogen requirements of crops will ultimately lead to a decline in soil productivity, and increased soil erosion.

When a change from a cropping system involving fallow to continuous cereal grain production, the nitrogen requirement increases. The nitrogen requirement is greatest in the first few years of continuous cropping as the nutrient cycling process adjusts to the new cropping system.

Crop Rotations

The value of forage crops in rotations with cereals and oilseeds has long been recognized, especially in the Luvisolic soils. Several long-term crop rotation studies conducted in Western Canada have shown that crop rotations involving perennial forages tend to stabilize soil organic matter at a higher level than crop rotations involving summer fallow.

Figure 5.2 summarises data obtained by the University of Alberta from the Breton Plots and the University of Manitoba. The Breton Plots compared a two-year fallow-wheat rotation with a five-year rotation involving wheat, oats and barley followed by two years of hay production.

In research done by the University of Manitoba, the effects of various cultural practices on the level of organic matter are compared. It is interesting to note that the highest level of soil organic matter was maintained under continuous cropping.

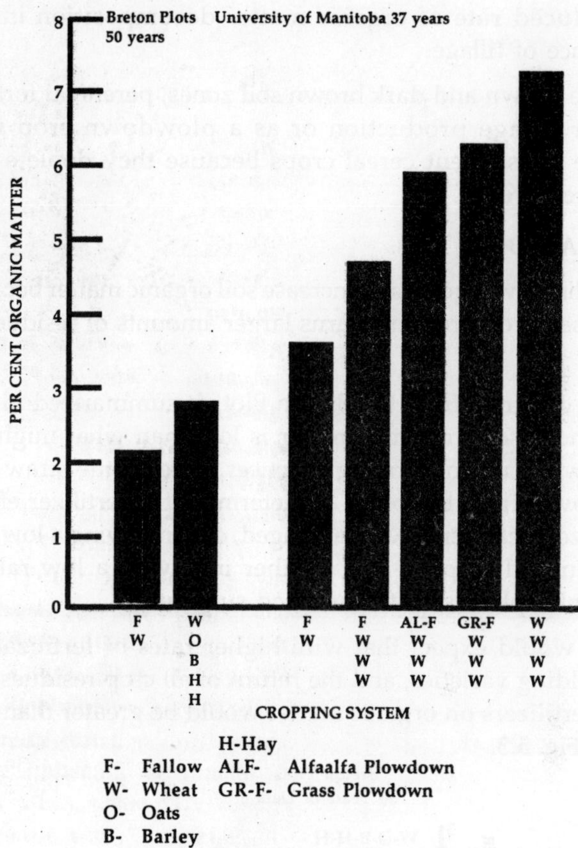

Fig. 5.2: Effect of rotation on soil organic matter

The beneficial effects of perennial forages are the result of:

- a more extensive root system and crop aftermath contributing more organic matter to the soil.
- the fibrous nature of the root system of perennial grasses. These are particularly effective as a binding agent in soil aggregation.
- Nitrogen fertility enhancement by the growth of legumes.

increased permeability of dense subsoils because of the deep penetrating tap roots of perennial legumes, especially alfalfa.

- a reduced rate of organic matter decomposition in the absence of tillage.

In the brown and dark brown soil zones, perennial forages grown for forage production or as a plowdown crop may jeopardize subsequent cereal crops because they deplete soil moisture reserves.

FERTILISATION

Fertilisers will generally increase soil organic matter because the increased crop growth returns larger amounts of residues to the soil.

Data obtained from the Breton Plots is summarized in Fig. 5.3. The increase in organic matter is less than what might be expected with current farming practices since all the straw had been removed from the plots. To determine the fertilizer effect, two fertilizer treatments were averaged, one involving a low rate of nitrogen and sulphur and another involving a low rate of nitrogen, phosphorus, potassium and sulphur.

One would expect that with higher rates of fertilization, higher yielding varieties, and the return of all crop residues, the effect of fertilizers on organic matter would be greater than that shown in Fig. 5.3.

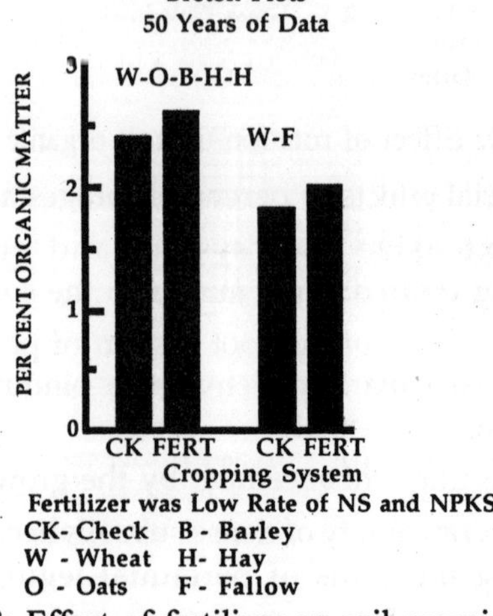

Fig. 5.3: Effect of fertilizer on soil organic matter

Plowdown

Legume plowdown has received considerable attention in recent years as an alternative to the use of nitrogen fertilizers. However, when considering this option in a cropping program, the amount of nitrogen added by the legume, as well as the loss of one year of production, the cost of seed and the expected yield increase must be kept in mind.

Strictly as a source of nitrogen, the value of a legume plowdown is questionable. The amount of nitrogen fixed by a legume is dependent upon the type of legume, the amount of vegetative growth, the nature of the soil and environmental conditions. As a source of organic matter, legume plowdown is valuable, however, perennial forage is more effective than legume plowdown for increasing soil organic matter.

Nitrate nitrogen which accumulates following legume plowdown is subject to loss, particularly in wet, poorly drained soils. To minimize this, legumes should be plowed down in the fall rather than mid-summer to reduce nitrate accumulation and subsequent loss.

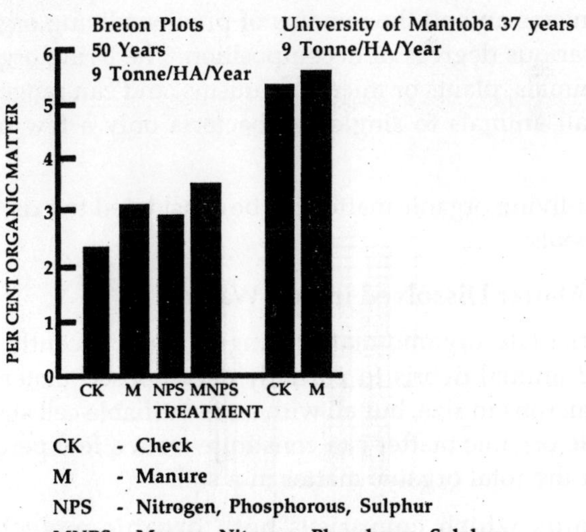

CK - Check

M - Manure

NPS - Nitrogen, Phosphorous, Sulphur

MNPS - Manure, Nitrogen, Phosphorus, Sulphur

Fig 5.4: Effect of manure on solid organic matter

The cultivation of prairie soils has generally resulted in a decline in organic matter of 30 to 50 per cent. A product of this decline has been the release of large amounts of plant nutrients, particularly nitrogen. Crop rotations with a high frequency of summerfallow have relied on the nitrogen released from soil organic matter to supply crop requirements.

More frequent or continuous cropping, less frequent tillage, the production of high yields and the return of crop residues will help to maintain soil organic matter at a satisfactory level. Perennial forages are effective for maintaining or increasing soil organic matter.

Organic matter is widely regarded as a vital component of a healthy soil. It is an important part of soil physical, chemical and biological fertility. This information examines what soil organic matter consists of and how it can contribute to soil fertility. It also discusses how soil management can affect organic matter concentrations in the long term, and presents evidence that addresses the question "how much organic matter does my soil need?"

In its broadest sense, soil organic matter comprises all living soil organisms and all the remains of previous living organisms in their various degrees of decomposition. The living organisms can be animals, plants or micro-organisms, and can range in size from small animals to single cell bacteria only a few microns long.

Non-living organic matter can be considered to exist in four distinct pools:

Organic Matter Dissolved in Soil Water

Particulate organic matter ranging from recently added plant and animal debris to partially decomposed material less than 50 microns in size, but all with an identifiable cell structure. Particulate organic matter can constitute from a few percent up to 25% of the total organic matter in a soil.

Humus which comprises both organic molecules of identifiable structure like proteins and cellulose, and molecules with no identifiable structure (humic and fulvic acids and humin) but which have reactive regions which allow the molecule to bond with other mineral and organic soil components . These molecules are moderate to large in size (molecular weights of 20,000-100,000). Humus usually represents the largest pool of soil organic matter, comprising over 50% of the total.

Inert organic matter or charcoal derived from the burning of plants. Can be up to 10% of the total soil organic matter.

When plant and animal debris is added to soil, it is broken down by macro- and micro-organisms, initially into particulate organic matter, and finally into humus. The raw materials can vary greatly in their resistance to breakdown. Woody organic substances like lignins are very resistant, while more simple compounds like sugars are readily utilised. Along the way, microbial populations increase. In the process they synthesise their own compounds which add to the diversity. In turn, these organisms die and are consumed by others.

Carbon dioxide is a by-product of this complex chain of processes (microbes breathe out CO_2 just like we do!). Over half of the carbon added to soil is lost as CO_2 during breakdown. Because of their varying reactivity, the turnover times for these different carbon fractions varies from a few months to tens of thousands of years.

MEASURING SOIL ORGANIC MATTER

While living organisms, particularly the plants we grow, are of vital importance to us, it is the non-living organic matter that we measure as 'soil organic matter'.

The most common methods for measuring soil organic matter in current use actually measure the amount of carbon in the soil. This is done by oxidising the carbon and measuring either the amount of oxidant used (wet oxidation, usually using dichromate) or the CO_2 given off in the process (combustion method with specific detection).

Laboratories these days generally report results as soil organic carbon. Those that report as soil organic matter have usually measured carbon and converted to organic matter by multiplying by 1.72. However, this conversion factor is not the same for all soils, and it is more precise to report soil carbon rather than organic matter.

The Amount of Organic Matter in Soil

The amount of carbon (the measure of organic matter) in a soil depends on a range of factors, and reflects the balance between accumulation and breakdown. The main factors are:

Climate: For similar soils under similar management, carbon is greater in areas of higher rainfall, and lower in areas of higher temperature. The rate of decomposition doubles for every 8 or 9°C increase in mean annual temperature. Tasmanian agricultural areas have a mean annual temperature of 11-13°C.

Soil type: Clay helps protect organic matter from breakdown, either by binding organic matter strongly or by forming a physical barrier which limits microbial access. Clay soils in the same area under similar management will tend to retain more carbon than sandy soils. Hence the sandy sodosols of the northern midlands have less carbon than the clay loam ferrosols of the north west regardless of management (Table 5.1).

Vegetative growth: The more vegetative production the greater are the inputs of carbon. Also, the more woody this vegetation is (greater C:N ratio), the slower it will breakdown. So, the crop system can strongly affect carbon concentrations.

Topography: Soils at the bottom of slopes generally have higher carbon because these areas are generally wetter and have higher clay contents. Poorly drained areas have much slower rates of carbon breakdown.

Tillage: Tillage will increase carbon breakdown. However, the impact of tillage is generally outweighed by the effect of management on the amount of carbon grown and returned to the soil. An exception to this is where tillage leads to increased erosion.

BENEFITS OF ORGANIC MATTER

Organic matter can be considered a pivotal component of the soil because of its role in physical, chemical and biological processes. Many of these functions interact. For example, the high cation exchange properties of organic matter are a major means by which organic matter is able to bind soil particles together in a more stable structure. The reactive regions present in humus are numerous, and give these molecules a capacity to bind to each other and to mineral soil particles, and also to react with cations (positive charge, e.g. Ca_2^+, K^+) in the soil solution.

The density of cation exchange capacity (CEC) of organic matter is greater than it is for clay minerals. While a high CEC is an important attribute of soil organic matter, please note that organic matter does not have an anion (negative) exchange capacity, and is therefore not able to bind anions like phosphate and sulphate. However, organic matter is a substantial reservoir for phosphorus and sulphur, as well as nitrogen. These elements are bound within the organic structure, and are released to the soil solution when microbes break down organic matter.

The ratio of carbon:nitrogen:sulphur:phosphorus in organic matter is roughly 100:10:1.5:1.5. A hectare of soil 10 cm deep with a bulk density of 1 tonne/m3 weighs 1,000,000 kg. Therefore, soil with a carbon content of 3% would contain 3,000 kg of organic nitrogen, and 450 kg each of organic phosphorus and sulphur per hectare. Not all of this is mineralised each year, but there is considerable potential for nutrients in organic matter to contribute to plant requirements. These should be taken into account, particularly the nitrogen.

Of all the components of soil, organic matter is probably the most important and most misunderstood. Organic matter serves as a reservoir of nutrients and water in the soil, aids in reducing compaction and surface crusting, and increases water infiltration into the soil. Yet it's often ignored and neglected. Let's examine the contributions of soil organic matter and talk about how to maintain or increase it.

Many times we think of organic matter as the plant and animal residues we incorporate into the soil. We see a pile of leaves, manure, or plant parts and think, "Wow! I'm adding a lot of organic matter to the soil." This stuff is actually organic material, not organic matter.

What's the difference between organic material and organic matter? Organic material is anything that was alive and is now in or on the soil. For it to become organic matter, it must be decomposed into humus. Humus is organic material that has been converted by microorganisms to a resistant state of decomposition. Organic material is unstable in the soil, changing form and mass readily as it decomposes. As much as 90 percent of it disappears quickly because of decomposition.

Organic matter is stable in the soil. It has been decomposed until it is resistant to further decomposition. Usually, only about 5 percent of it mineralizes yearly. That rate increases if temperature, oxygen, and moisture conditions become favorable for decomposition, which often occurs with excessive tillage. It is the stable organic matter that is analyzed in the soil test.

How Much Organic Matter is in the Soil?

An acre of soil measured to a depth of 6 inches weighs approximately 2,000,000 pounds, which means that 1 percent organic matter in the soil would weigh about 20,000 pounds per acre. Remember that it takes at least 10 pounds of organic material to decompose to 1 pound of organic matter, so it takes at least 200,000 pounds (100 tons) of organic material applied or returned to the soil to add 1 percent stable organic matter under favorable conditions.

In soils that formed under prairie vegetation, organic-matter levels are generally comparatively high because organic material was supplied from both the top growth and the roots. We don't usually think of roots as supplying organic material, but a study in the Upper Great Plains showed that a mixed prairie had an above-ground (shoot) yield of 1.4 tons of organic material per acre, while the root yield was about 4 tons per acre. The plants were producing roots that were more than twice the weight of the shoots.

Soils that have developed under forest vegetation usually have comparably low organic-matter levels. There are at least two reasons for these levels: (1) trees produce a much smaller root mass per acre than grass plants, and (2) trees do not die back and decompose every year. Instead, much of the organic material in a forest is tied up in the tree instead of being returned to the soil.

Soils that formed under prairie vegetation usually have native organic matter levels at least twice as high as those formed under forest vegetation.

Nutrient Supply

Organic matter is a reservoir of nutrients that can be released to the soil. Each percent of organic matter in the soil releases 20 to 30 pounds of nitrogen, 4.5 to 6.6 pounds of P2O5, and 2 to 3 pounds of sulfur per year. The nutrient release occurs predominantly in the spring and summer, so summer crops benefit more from organic-matter mineralization than winter crops.

Water-Holding Capacity

Organic matter behaves somewhat like a sponge, with the ability to absorb and hold up to 90 percent of its weight in water. A great advantage of the water-holding capacity of organic matter is that the matter will release most of the water that it absorbs to plants. In contrast, clay holds great quantities of water, but much of it is unavailable to plants.

Soil Structure Aggregation

Organic matter causes soil to clump and form soil aggregates, which improves soil structure. With better soil structure, permeability (infiltration of water through the soil) improves, in turn improving the soil's ability to take up and hold water.

Erosion Prevention

This property of organic matter is not widely known. Data used in the universal soil loss equation indicate that increasing soil organic matter from 1 to 3 percent can reduce erosion 20 to 33 percent because of increased water infiltration and stable soil aggregate formation caused by organic matter.

Building soil organic matter is a long-term process but can be beneficial. Here are a few ways to do it.

Reduce or Eliminate Tillage

Tillage improves the aeration of the soil and causes a flush of microbial action that speeds up the decomposition of organic matter. Tillage also often increases erosion. No-till practices can help build organic matter.

Reduce Erosion

Most soil organic matter is in the topsoil. When soil erodes, organic matter goes with it. Saving soil and soil organic matter go hand in hand.

Soil-Test and Fertilize Properly

You may not have considered this one. Proper fertilization encourages growth of plants, which increases root growth. Increased root growth can help build or maintain soil organic matter, even if you are removing much of the top growth.

Cover Crops

Growing cover crops can help build or maintain soil organic matter. However, best results are achieved if growing cover crops is combined with tillage reduction and erosion control measures.

A good supply of soil organic matter is beneficial in crop or forage production. Consider the benefits of this valuable resource and how you can manage your operation to build, or at least maintain, the organic matter in your soil

Vegetables, flowers and landscape plants grown in soil that is high in organic matter often are damaged less by nematodes than are plants in soil of low organic matter content. Any kind of organic soil amendment, including compost, green manures, and lightly incorporated organic mulches, can have this effect. Organic amendments both improve tolerance of the plant host and apparently reduce nematode populations. However, they can not magically eliminate a severe nematode infestation overnight. They are better suited to keeping nematode populations relatively low than reducing high ones. There are several ways in which organic soil amendments may help reduce nematode injury to plants.

Soil organic matter is any material in the soil that was originally produced by living organisms. At any given time, it consists of a range of materials varying from the intact original tissues of plants (mainly) and animals to the substantially decomposed mixture of mate.

In a soil which at first has no readily decomposable materials, adding fresh tissue under favorable conditions immediately starts rapid multiplication of bacteria, fungi, and actinomycetes, which aresoon actively decomposing the fresh tissue. As the most readiy available energy sources (carbohydrates, fats, proteins) are used up, those microorganisms again become relatively inactive, leaving behind a dark mixture usually referred to as humus. Newly-formed humus is a combination of resistant materials from the original plant tissue and compounds synthesized as part of the microorganisms' tissue which remain as the organisms die. It is quite resistant to further microbial attack, so its nitrogen and other essential nutrients are protected from ready solubility and dissipation.

Humus holds water and minerals extremely well; it sticks together very well, so helps soil establish and maintain a strong crumb struture; it provides some nutrients as it is slowly decayed by microbial activity.

ADDING ORGANIC MATTER TO SOIL

We can add organic matter to soil in several forms, including:

- *compost* — organic material that has been substantially decomposd under somewhat controlled conditions, so that most of the readily-exploited nutrients are exhausted.
- *undecomposed plant and animal material* — often leaves and garden waste that were set aside at clean-up or harvest (e.g., fresh pine straw and sawdust).
- *green manure* — fresh plant material grown purposely to be incorporated into the soil on the site where it was grown while it is lush.

Compost will provide mineral nutrients plants need, and be converted into humus. Since the readily-available nutrients are mostly consumed in the composting process, compost will not stimulate activity of the same kinds of microorganisms as will fresh tissue, nor the amount of microbial activity.

Whole, but not fresh, organic matter has any of the nutrients that fresh green material has, but must have moisture added for decomposition to proceed. Many sugars, starches, etc. become available for microbial use more slowly once the material has had a chance to dry out, so the decomposition process takes longer. Older tissues often contain less of those readily-available nutrients, and more of those that are present are tied up in complex compounds that are resistant to microbial attack.

Green manuring (discussed in detail below) is turning under of a green crop to better the condition of the soil. Material so added, if soil is in proper condition and well managed, can help maintain or raise the organic matter content of the soil, and thus its ability to produce crops, in several ways.

Humus and partly decomposed soil organic matter can greatly increase the water- and nutrient-holding capacities of sandy soils, reducing some of the major stresses which magnify the effects of nematode damage to roots. Mulches of organic materials which help keep roots cool and reduce evaporation from soil also help reduce stress, and add humus as they decompose.

Soil Biological Activity

Decomposing organic matter is food for many soil microbes (fungi, actinomycetes, and bacteria). Some of those creatures are natural enemies of plant nematodes; increasing their numbers enhances "natural" nematode control.

Chemical By-Products

Decomposition of some organic amendments, including some green manures and oily plant residues such as cottonseed meal, has been shown to release chemicals which are directly toxic to nematodes. Those chemicals may reduce nematode numbers directly, in addition to the other benefits derived from soil organic amendments.

"Nematicidal" Miracle Products

Claims of nematode control are made for many products sold as soil amendments and additives, but objective research data rarely accompany those claims. If a product's claims cannot be supported with evidence from well-designed research, preferably conducted by scientists who are in no way connected with the product, be very cautious about depending on it for nematode control.

GREEN MANURES

Green manuring is the practice of growing lush plants on the site into which you wish to incorporate organic matter, then turning (tilling, plowing, spading) it into the soil while it is still fresh. The plant material used in this way is called a green manure. The plant material may or may not be cut free from its roots before being incorporated into the soil, depending on what is needed to be able to handle it. Green manuring is popular among "pure" organic gardeners and farmers; it is equally appreciated by many farmers who use some practices that are not acceptable to organic enthusiasts. It is widely adopted simply because adding large amounts of green plant material benefits many soil characteristics, including drainage and water retention, nutrient content and form of storage, and level of microbiological activity in the soil.

- Green manuring supplies soil organic matter, as already discussed.
- It can conserve or even add nutrients. Nitrogen used by the green manure crop has been protected from leaching loss and microbial degradation that could take place if the land were left fallow. Other nutrients such as potassium, phosphorus, magnesium, and iron can be similarly conserved through green manuring. Using a legume can increase soil nitrogen levels through N fixation by the Rhizobium bacteria associated with most legume roots.
- Microbiological benefits—there is a substantial increase in activity of soil fungi and bacteria that do many useful things. Generally, the more diverse and greater the soil microbial population, the more productive the soil will be.

- Conservation of top-soil against loss by erosion can be a substantial nutrient conservation benefit of green manuring.

Green manuring has also been demonstrated to reduce levels of nematodes in the soil in some cases, in addition to reducing the sensitivity of plants to modest levels of nematode injury by improving the soil environment of their roots.

To be useful as a green manure, a plant should: (1) grow rapidly; (2) produce abundant and succulent tops; (3) grow well in the conditions of the site. The higher the moisture content of the material, the more rapidly will it break down and its benefits be realized. When other conditions are equal, it is better to use a legume because of the nitrogen fixation and the microbial activity it promotes.

Crops that are selected for use as green manures are usually chosen for their ability to grow very rapidly and produce a large mass of top growth at the season and site. Cool season grasses are often used in Florida for fall and winter green manure crops; legumes are often desirable because they naturally convert nitrogen from the air into plant nutrients, thus increasing the levels of that most critical nutrient in the soil when the plant tissues are incorporated into the soil.

It is generally best to turn green crops under when their succulence is near the maximum, yet when enough top growth has been produced; this is often at or slightly past the half-mature stage.

If a "nematicidal" crop such as those discussed below can be used as a green manure, it may have an even greater effect on nematodes in the soil, by beginning their reduction as a cover crop before it is turned into the soil. For instance, hairy indigo is valuable in both ways in North and Central Florida.

Risks in Green Manuring

Take care to avoid planting green manure crops that can encourage reproduction of nematodes, especially root-knot nematodes. Increasing a nematode population on a green manure crop canoffset all benefits that would otherwise be gained. If at all possible, choose crops for green manuring that are known to inhibit root knot nematodes.

CHAPTER–6
Soil Colloids

INTRODUCTION

The soil colloids are the most active portion of the soil and largely determine the physical and chemical properties of a soil. Inorganic colloids (clay minerals, hydrous oxides) usually make up the bulk of soil colloids. Colloids are particles less than 0.001 mm in size, and the clay fraction includes particles less than 0.002 mm in size. Therefore, all clay minerals are not strictly colloidal. The organic colloids include highly decomposed organic matter generally called humus. Organic colloids are more reactive chemically and generally have a greater influence on soil properties per unit weight than the inorganic colloids. Humus is amorphous and its chemical and physical characteristics are not well defined. Clay minerals are usually crystalline (although some are amorphous) and usually have a characteristic chemical and physical configuration. Both inorganic and organic colloids are intimately mixed with other soil solids. Thus, the bulk of the soil solids are essentially inert and the majority of the soil's physical and chemical character is a result of the colloids present.

CATION EXCHANGE

One of the most important properties of colloids is their ability to adsorb, hold, and release ions. Colloids generally have a net negative charge as a result of their physical and chemical composition. This negative charge is balanced by thousands of cations. Thus, colloids can be viewed as huge anions surrounded by a swarm of rather loosely held cations. Water molecules are also adsorbed to colloid surfaces; they are present as part of the hydrated structure of the cations. The amount of water associated with a particular cation is important, because the effective radius of the cation changes with the amount of hydration, or associated water.

In humid regions, the cations associated with the colloids are dominated by Ca^{+2}, H^+, and often $A1^{+3}$, resulting in acidic soils. As the soil becomes more acid, H^+ and Al^{+3} become more predominant. The cations Mg^{+2}, K^+, and Na^+ are usually found in lesser amounts, while NH_4^+ may be present in considerable quantities if the soil has been recently fertilized with ammonium fertilizers. In semiarid and arid regions, Ca^{2+} usually dominated the cations, but Mg^{2+} and N^{a+} are often found in large quantities. H^+ and $A1^{3+}$ are usually present only in small concentrations.

Many of the other plant nutrient cations are found only in very small amounts as cations on colloidal surfaces. More often, they are found as chelates or in chemical combination. Such cations include Mn^{+2}, Zn^{+2}, Cu^{+2}, Fe^{+2}, and Fe^{+3} and generally make up only a small percent of the exchangeable cations. Anionic nutrients, such as NO_3^-, C_1^-, SO_4^{-2}, and PO_4^{-3} are not held on the surfaces of colloids to any great extent. Instead, they exist as free anions in the soil solution or fixed within chemical compounds.

Cation exchange is the exchange of a cation in the soil solution for another on the surface of a colloid. Cation exchange is a phenomena which is constantly going in soils and is of great importance. Without some mechanism to temporarily hold cations in the soil, plants would be unable to obtain sufficient quantities of the essential nutrients to grow. Without cation exchange, the nutrients would simply be leached downward in the soil and lost. Cation exchange plays a role in other soil processes as well. Acidification is the process of exchanging basic cations, such as Ca^{+2}, Mg^{+2}, K^+, and Na^+, for acidic cations, such as H^+ and Al^{+3}. Liming acid soils results in a reversal of this process, H^+ ions are exchanged for Ca^{+2} ions. If cationic fertilizer nutrients are not held by the soil colloids, the nutrients would be lost to percolation water.

Cation exchange capacity (CEC) is a quantitative measure of the ability of a soil to exchange cations with the soil solution and is expressed in terms of cmols(+) kg^{-1} of soil. Historically, soil scientists have expressed CEC in terms of meq/100 g of soil and these units were often encountered in textbooks and journal articles. The unit cmol kg^{-1} is equal to meg/100 g.

The cmol weight of the ions commonly found in soils is easily calculated by knowing:

1. the relative atomic mass of the ion divided by 100;and
2. the charge on the ion.

For example, the calcium ion has a relative atomic mass of 40 g mol^{-1} or 0.40 g $cmol^{-1}$ and a charge of two. Because if it's charge, it will replace 2 of hydrogen (hydrogen has a charge of 1) atoms. Dividing the relative atomic mass of the ion by its charge gives you the cmol weight of the ion. For Ca^{2+}, that is 40 g mol^{-1} or 0.40 g $cmol^{-1}$/2 or 0.20 g $cmol^{-1}$.

Table 6.1: Relative atomic mass, charge, and cmol weight for some common soil ions

Relative *Ion*	*Atomic* *mass charge*	*cmol weight* *g/cmol^{-1}*
Al^{+3}	27	+3 0.09
Ca^{+2}	40	+2 0.20
Cl^{-1}	35	-1 0.35
CO^{-2}	60	-2 0.30
H^{+3}	1	+1 0.01
K^{+}	39	+1 0.39
Mg^{+2}	24	+2 0.12
Na^{+}	23	+1 0.23
NH_{4-}	+18	+1 0.18
NO_{3-2}	62	-1 0.62
SO_{4}	96	-2 0.48
ZN^{+2}	65	+2 0.32.5

Cation exchange capacity (CEC) is an expression of the 'amount' of cations held in the soil. This is expressed as cmol of cations per kg of soil. When the CEC is combined with the cmol weight of a particular cation, then the 'amount' of that cation can be expressed on a weight basis. Three examples of this are given below for H^+, Ca^{2+}, and Al^{3+}, respectively.

Assume a soil has a CEC of 20 cmol kg^{-1} g of soil (this means that 1 kg of soil will hold 20 cmol (the 'amount') of cations. To convert this 'amount' of cations to a weight basis, the cmol weight (g $cmol^{-1}$) is multiplied by the CEC, as follows:

Assume all of the exchange sites are occupied by:

H^+:

CEC × cmol wgt = 'amount' of cation on weight basis

$$\frac{20\text{ cmol}}{1\text{ kg soil}} \times \frac{.01\text{g H}^+}{1\text{ cmol H}^+} = .20\text{g H}^+,\text{kg}^{-1}\text{soil}$$

Ca2+:

CEC × cmol wgt = 'amount' of cation on weight basis

$$\frac{20\text{ cmol}}{1\text{ kg soil}} \times \frac{.20\text{ g Ca}^{+2}}{1\text{ cmol Ca}^{+2}} = 4.00\text{ g Ca}^{+2}\text{ kg}^{-1}\text{soil}$$

A13+:

CEC × cmol wgt = 'amount' of cation on weight basis

$$\frac{20\text{ cmol}}{1\text{ kg soil}} \times \frac{.09\text{ g Al}^{+3}}{1\text{ cmol Al}^{+3}} = 4.60\text{ Al}^{+3}\text{ kg}^{-1}\text{soil}$$

Another calculation often required is the conversion of 'amount' in soil on a weight basis from (g kg^{-1} soil) to (pounds/acre furrow slice) or (kilograms/hectare 15 cm). Remembering that an acre furrow slice weighs 2 million pounds, we can say that pounds of nutrient per acre furrow slice is the same as parts per 2 million (pp2m). The next step is the conversion of g kg soil to ppm. Assume that a soil will hold .400 g of Ca^{+2} kg of soil. To calculate how much Ca^{+2} that could exist in the soil (expressed as pounds per acre furrow slice) (1b/AFS), first convert CEC to ppm, as follows:

$$\frac{0.400\text{ g Ca}^{+2}}{1\text{ kg}} \times \frac{1{,}000{,}000\text{ kg}}{1{,}000{,}000\text{ kg}} = \frac{4{,}000\text{ kg}}{1{,}000{,}000\text{ kg}} = 4000\text{ ppm}$$

Then change ppm to pp^2m or pounds per acre furrow slice as follows:

4000 ppm × 2 = 8000 pp^2m or 8000 lbs/AFS

The conversion of g of nutrient kg^{-1} soil to kg ha^{-1} is similar. A hectar furrow slice (15 cm deep) weighs 2,000,000 kg.

FLOCCULATION AND DISPERSION

Soils are generally in an aggregated state. Aggregation, however, is dependent on the soil colloids and the cations associated with them. Soil colloids can be in either a flocculated or dispersed state. The normal situation is for colloids to be in a flocculated state. Individual particles stick together to form aggregates of particles or floccules. Such aggregates do not move in the soil solution and form the basis for soil structure. When soil particles are dispersed, aggregates do not form, and each particle behaves as an individual. Without aggregation, water, air, and root movement in the soil is inhibited. Thus, dispersion is not a desirable characteristic of productive soils.

The type of cations present in the soil solution determines whether a soil is dispersed or flocculated. Sodium cations cause dispersion while calcium, magnesium, aluminum, and hydrogen ions promote flocculation. Because colloids are simply large anions, they attract cations in order to neutralize their negative charge. Flocculating cations sufficiently neutralize the negative charge, allowing colloids to adhere and flocculate. The attraction of particular cations to the negatively charged colloids is a function of two things, the hydrated size of the cation and the charge of the cation. These two factors combine to determine the charge density on the cation, in other words, the distribution of charge over the surface of the cation. For example, with the highly hydrated Na^+ cation, the hydrated size of the cation is relatively large, while its charge is only +1. So, that +1 charge has to be distributed over a relatively large area. With such a large cation having such a low charge, the negative charge on the colloids is not sufficiently satisfied and the colloids actually repel one another, resulting in dispersion.

SHRINKING AND SWELLING

Soils shrink and swell as they dry and rewet. Shrinking and swelling is an important factor in the construction of bridges, roads, and buildings, because of the pressures exerted by swelling or expanding soils on the foundations of such structures. Shrinking and swelling is largely a function of the type of colloid present, particularly clay colloids. As water moves in and out of clay crystal lattices, they respond by expanding or contracting. Extreme expansion and contraction is exhibited by clays such as montmorillonite, which have expanding lattices. Clays with nonexpanding lattices, such as kaolinite and chlorite, have very little capacity to shrink and swell.

The exercises that follow contain a hypothesis relating to the concepts presented in the above discussion. Each hypothesis is followed by a simple experiment designed to test that hypothesis. The results of each experiment should be viewed qualitatively and evaluated as to whether they validate the hypothesis.

CHAPTER–7

Trace Elements in the Soil

INTRODUCTION

Although they are only needed by plants and animals in very small amounts, trace elements are nonetheless essential for healthy growth. The trace elements of interest in agriculture include the following:

- Boron Iodine
- Molybdenum
- Cobalt
- Iron
- Selenium
- Copper
- Manganese
- Zinc

BORON

Boron has the chemical symbol B, and is found in soil solution in the form of boric acid (H_3BO_3). As it is predominately in this soluble form, boron is vulnerable to loss by leaching, which is particularly a problem on sandy soils.

However, boron can also bind onto soil organic matter and clay particles, and this offers some protection from leaching loss. This bound boron is slowly released and enters the soil solution.

The release of boron complexed to soil organic matter can be accelerated by the addition of lime. This stimulates microbial activity, which hastens organic matter breakdown, so speeding up the release of boron. Conversely, the release of boron is inhibited by dry conditions, as this slows microbial activity, and hence reduces the rate at which organic matter is degraded.

In addition, soil pH affects the availability of boron. At low pH (less than 5.0) boron complexes with iron and aluminium oxides on soil surfaces, making it unavailable for plant use. Soils with an alkaline pH (above 7.0) can also suffer from boron deficiencies.

COBALT

Cobalt has the chemical symbol Co, and is found in soil predominately as a divalent ion (Co^{2+}) and also as a trivalent ion (Co^{3+}).

The availability of cobalt in soil is influenced mainly by soil pH. In soils of very low pH cobalt is oxidised to the trivalent ion and is often found associated with iron. As the pH rises, the divalent ion becomes predominant. Once soil reaches pH 6 to 7, there is a greater tendency for cobalt to become adsorbed on to soil colloids, which means it is less available to plants.

Applying lime to soil can result in lower cobalt availability. This is thought to be because the presence of lime causes manganese to precipitate out of solution, and this manganese then reacts with cobalt to form insoluble compounds.

Cobalt is also subject to loss by leaching, and there is generally lower cobalt availability in free-draining soils (and higher availability in waterlogged soils) as a result.

In New Zealand, four regions are particularly vulnerable to cobalt deficiency. They are:

- Northland's highly weathered and sandy soils.
- The rhyolitic ash-based yellow-brown pumice soils of the Central Plateau.

- Nelson's granite-derived yellow-brown earth soils.
- The southern yellow-brown earths derived from sedimentary rocks in Southland.

COPPER

Copper (chemical symbol Cu) is found in a wide range of soil materials, including limestones, igneous rocks, sandstones and shales. How much of this copper makes its way into the soils formed from these parent materials depends on a wide range of factors, including the degree of weathering of the rock, the amount of drainage, the amount of organic material in the soil, pH and oxidation-reduction potential.

Under alkaline conditions, copper in soil tends to precipitate out of solution, so availability is reduced. When the soil is acidic, copper becomes more soluble, so the concentration in soil solution rises.

In New Zealand, copper deficiency is most frequently seen on peats, podzols (for example, the Northland gumland soils), yellow-brown pumice soils derived from rhyolite ash, coastal sands, some yellow-grey earths derived from greywacke loess, and limestone soils with high pH.

IODINE

Iodine has the chemical symbol I and is most abundant in igneous rocks, seawater, seaweed and Chilean saltpetre. In soil, iodine occurs as iodine (I^-), iodate (IO^{3-}) and organically bound iodine.

Of these, the reduced form of iodine (I^-) is relatively mobile in soil, whereas iodate is relatively immobile, as it can be sorbed onto soil compounds. Organically bound iodine is generally regarded as inaccessible, unless released by microbial activity.

In New Zealand, low concentrations of iodine occur in brown-grey earths derived from schist and greywacke, in yellow-grey earths derived from greywacke, loess and alluvium, and also in the yellow-brown pumice soils.

IRON

Iron has the chemical symbol Fe, which reflects its Latin name, ferrum. It is the second most abundant metal in earth's crust, with about 5 per cent of the earth's core estimated to be iron.

In New Zealand, soils that are low in iron include podzols, organic soils and soils derived from silica-rich rocks such as granite. In contrast, high iron concentrations are found in strongly weathered brown and red loams derived from basaltic scoria, and in brown granular clays derived from andesite.

In soil, iron exists in the ferrous (Fe^{2+}) and ferric (Fe^{3+}) forms. The ferric forms have low solubility in soil solution, so when these predominate, iron availability decreases. When ferrous forms are predominant, iron availability is increased.

An alkaline soil pH increases the amount of ferric iron in the soil, and so means that iron availability is low. As a result, iron deficiency can be triggered by heavy use of lime. However, most soils in New Zealand – especially those used for pastoral agriculture – have a pH less than 6.5, so iron availability is not a concern.

The presence of organic matter in soil improves iron availability. This is because the iron combines with the organic matter, which means it is not fixed or precipitated as ferric hydroxide, processes that both reduce the availability of iron. Iron that is incorporated in organic matter is released by microbial activity. In acid soils this increase in microbial activity can cause a reduction in the level of oxygen in soils, which helps drive iron from the poorly soluble ferric forms to the soluble ferrous forms, so increasing iron availability.

MANGANESE

Manganese has the chemical symbol Mn, and minerals containing manganese are widely distributed throughout the earth. As a result, most soils contain substantial amounts of manganese. However, in New Zealand, low concentrations of manganese are found in the strongly leached podzols of the West Coast of the South Island and Northland, and most peat soils.

Manganese deficiencies can occur, though, and these usually occur because the manganese is in a form that cannot be taken up by plants. Soil pH is the main driver of such conditions, as alkaline pH causes the concentration of the divalent manganese ion (Mn^{2+}) to fall. This is more extreme in soils with high organic matter contents, since the Mn^{2+} ions form complexes with the organic matter. Manganese deficiencies can also occur when soils become dry, as this can promote the formation of dehydrated manganese salts, which are not available for plant uptake.

Manganese becomes very soluble once the pH is 5.5 or lower and in some instances this can result in manganese toxicity. In addition, manganese solubility is also enhanced when soils are waterlogged, as soil bacteria can then reduce manganese oxide to Mn^{2+}, increasing the availability of manganese.

MOLYBDENUM

Molybdenum has the chemical symbol Mo, and is typically present in soils at a concentration of 2 mg/kg (worldwide average). In nature, molybdenum occurs as iron molybdates, the molybdenum being released by weathering.

Many soils in New Zealand are deficient in molybdenum, including the podzols, some yellow-grey earths and all yellow-brown earths derived from greywacke.

The availability of molybdenum increases as soil pH increases. In acid soils, especially those with a pH of less than 5.5, deficiencies occur. At these lower pH levels, the prevalence of aluminium and iron increases, and these two elements tend to bind with molybdenum and form insoluble complexes.

Molybdenum attaches quite strongly to clay particles and organic matter in soils, and this protects it from being lost by leaching. In this respect, it is similar to phosphate.

SELENIUM

Selenium is named after the Greek word for the moon, selene, and carries the chemical symbol Se. It is found in very low concentrations in igneous rocks, shales, sandstones and limestones, and is emitted in volcanic eruptions along with sulphur.

The naturally low levels of selenium in soil mean deficiencies can be an issue, and in New Zealand about 30 percent of land is affected by this. Sandy soils, including the sandy pumice soils, are most affected, as are semi-arid soils and pallic soils formed on loess in the South Island.

Before selenium can be used by plants it needs to be oxidised to a form that is able to be taken up by the plant roots. This can be achieved by a wide range of complex biogeochemical reactions, and may also be mediated by organic acids exuded by plant roots.

ZINC

Zinc has the chemical symbol Zn and it occurs in a range of minerals, with the average concentration in the earth's crust estimated at 40 mg/kg. Zinc deficiency in pastures is virtually unknown in New Zealand.

Total zinc levels tend to be higher in clay soils and lower in sandy soils and peat soils, but the availability of this zinc is moderated by both soil pH and soil organic matter content.

As soil pH rises, the availability of zinc declines, and as a result of this a zinc deficiency can be induced by overliming. In addition, plant-available zinc is associated with organic matter, so soils low in organic matter are more prone to zinc deficiencies.

CHAPTER–8
Soil Test

INTRODUCTION

In agriculture, a soil test is the analysis of a soil sample to determine nutrient content, composition and other characteristics, including contaminants. Tests are usually performed to measure fertility and indicate deficiencies that need to be remedied.

Soil Sampling

The quality of the original soil sample plays a key role in determining the practical value of test results. Most labs will provide documentation outlining the proper procedures for collecting soil samples.

Labs, such as Iowa State and Colorado State University, recommend that you take between 10-20 samples for every 40 acres (160,000 m^2) of the field. Sampling implements must be properly cleaned prior to sampling, and must be cleaned between samples to avoid cross-contamination (especially when sampling and testing for soil contaminants). The tool should be free of rust, and washed with distilled water. Doing so will clean the tool, but also not add any minerals or elements from regular tap water or chemicals that could change the composition of the soil.

Soil characteristics can vary significantly from one spot to another, even in a small garden or field. Taking samples everywhere in the field is crucial to get the most accurate measurement of nutrients and other organisms. An example of this is along gravel roads where the soil could have more lime from the dust from the roads settling down in the soil, or an old animal feedlot where phosphorus and nitrogen counts could be higher than the rest of the field.

Sample depth is also an important factor. It is recommended that you take the samples from tillage depth, as this is where the majority of the nutrients and elements are placed mechanically. The presence of various nutrients and other soil components varies during the year, so sample timing may also be important. A good time to take a sample for testing is in the fall after harvesting is finished, but this isn't the only time it should be done.

Sampling and testing in the fall is beneficial because the producer will get the results back in time to formulate the fertilizer plan for the following growing season. Another time sampling and testing can be done is spring. This is a good way to see what nutrients survive over winter when the soil freezes, as well as if any leeches away from melting of snow and thawing of the soil. This way the producer can know if more or less fertilizer needs to be purchased.

Mixing soil from several locations to create an "average" (or "composite") sample is a common procedure but it must be used judiciously as it can artificially dilute quantities/ concentrations of soil components and may not meet government agency requirements for sampling. Make a reference map for your filing system so you know where you took them, and how many samples you took in the field. All of these considerations affect the interpretation of test results.

STORAGE AND HANDLING

Because certain characteristics of soil change with time it is essential that soil is analyzed as soon as practical. If it can not be tested within 24 hours of sampling soil should be frozen to reduce changes due to biological and chemical activity. Longer periods between sampling and testing may require the soil to be air dried. Properly dried soil may be stable for periods of 6 months or more.

Soil Testing

Soil testing is often performed by commercial labs that offer an extensive array of specific tests. Choosing the test lab site is just as important as the test results. There are many soil testing labs in the United States, but finding the right one for you will take some research. It is most beneficial for the producer to find the local most lab, as the workers will have a greater knowledge and more experience working with the local soils.

Tests include, but aren't limited to, major nutrients—nitrogen (N), phosphorus (P), and potassium (K), secondary nutrients - sulphur, calcium, magnesium, minor nutrients - iron, manganese, copper, zinc, boron, molybdenum, aluminum, physical properties—soil acidity, electrical conductivity, soil organic matter, moisture content, and soil contaminants (e.g., fuel components such as benzene, toluene, xylene, petroleum hydrocarbons).

Soil testing can be an easy, cost effective way to manage agronomic as well as horticultural soils. It tells key nutrient levels, as well as pH levels, so the producer can make the best choice when purchasing fertilizers and other nutrients.

New prepaid mail-in kits have come to market that offer two specific benefits to small acreage farmers, urban homewoners and the lawn care industry: first is an inexpensive and quick manner to transfer soil samples directly to an accreditted laboratory for analysis; and second, the process translates raw data findings into workable and practical nutrient management/ fertilizer reports. One such kit can be viewed at [http:www.grass-roots.ca]. This particular process provides an actual 'prescrition' of fertilizers that are readily available in the global market for two complete seasons.

Less comprehensive do-it-yourself kits are also available, usually with tests for three important plant nutrients—nitrogen (N), phosphorus (P), and potassium (K) — and for soil acidity (pH). Do-it-yourself kits can usually be purchased at your local cooperative or through the university or private lab you choose. Prices of the tests will vary on the lab/university you purchase it from and also on what kind of test you want to do. Lab tests are more accurate, though both types are useful. In addition, lab tests frequently include professional interpretation of results and recommendations. Always refer to all proviso statements included in a lab report — these may outline any anomalies, exceptions and shortcomings in the sampling and/or analytical process/results.

Gardening

Home gardens use soil testing both for pH and nutrient analysis (Extractable Nutrients: P, K, Ca, Mg, Fe, Mn, Zn, Cu, B), and to determine contaminant levels, particularly for lead: Extractable Heavy Metals (Pb, Cd, Ni, Cr).

"Background concentrations of lead that occur naturally in surface agricultural soils in the United States average 10 parts per million (ppm) with a range of 7 to 20 ppm. Soils with lead levels above this range are primarily the result of lead contamination. There are two major sources of lead contamination: (1) lead-based paint where contamination may occur when paint chips from old buildings mix with the soil; and (2) lead from auto emissions. Studies conducted in urban areas, have shown that soil lead levels are highest around building foundations and within a few feet of busy streets.

"The most serious source of exposure to soil lead is through direct ingestion (eating) of contaminated soil or dust. In general, plants do not absorb or accumulate lead. However, in soils testing high in lead, it is possible for some lead to be taken up. Studies have shown that lead does not readily accumulate in the fruiting parts of vegetable and fruit crops (e.g., corn, beans, squash, tomatoes, strawberries, apples). Higher concentrations are more likely to be found in leafy vegetables (e.g., lettuce) and on the surface of root crops (e.g., carrots)."

Lead Level/Extracted Lead (ppm)/Estimated Total Lead (ppm)

Low/less than 43/less than 500*

Medium/43 to 126/500 to 1000

High/126 to 480/1000 to 3000

Very High/greater than 480/greater than 3000

(*) If estimated total soil lead levels are above 300 ppm, however, young children and pregnant women should avoid soil contact.

Good Gardening Practices to Reduce the Lead Risk

1. Locate gardens away from old painted structures and heavily traveled roads.
2. Give planting preferences to fruiting crops (tomatoes, squash, peas, sunflowers, corn, etc.).
3. Incorporate organic materials such as finished compost, humus, and peat moss.
4. Lime soil as recommended by soil test (pH 6.5 minimizes lead availability).
5. Discard old and outer leaves before eating leafy vegetables. Peel root crops. Wash all produce.
6. Keep dust to a minimum by maintaining a mulched and/ or moist soil surface.

HOW TO TAKE SOIL SAMPLES

To have a soil analysis done you need to collect 12 or more cores which will be combined as one composite sample. The samples should include soil from the surface to a depth of 6 inches in all areas except for lawns where cores should be taken from a depth of only 2 to 3 inches. A simple garden trowel can be used to collect the samples. Place the samples in a clean bucket and mix them thoroughly. It is imperative to use clean sampling tools. Pesticide or fertilizer residues will create misleading results. The sample must not be excessively wet before it goes to the lab. Bring a minimum of 2 cups of soil per sample to your county Extension office. Be sure to keep track of which part of your yard the sample came from. At the Extension office they will ask you to fill out the information on a soil test box, fill out a record sheet and check the appropriate boxes for the analyses desired. The cost of a standard soil test is $6.00 per sample. This test provides unbiased, scientific information on:

THE SOIL pH VALUE

The current soil levels of phosphorus, potassium, calcium, magnesium, zinc and manganese.

Fertiliser and lime recommendations (if needed) for the plants you are growing.

How Many Samples to Take

You need to take a soil sample from each section of your yard or garden. Usually this means, for example, one sample in your turf area, one in any foundation or perennial bed and one in your vegetable garden. If you have a problem area where plants do not seem to grow well, take a separate soil sample from that location.

Sampling Frequency

The Clemson University Extension Service recommends soil sampling every year.

Time of Sampling

Soil samples can be taken at any time of the year, but it is best to sample the soil a couple months before planting a garden, establishing perennials or before the optimum time for fertilizing lawns to allow ample time for the lime to react with the soil.

Soil Test Results

Within seven to fourteen days, a copy of your soil analysis will be mailed directly to you from the Agricultural Service Lab. Your county Extension office will also receive a copy. Your soil analysis will have a bar graph representing the amount of soil nutrients found and the soil pH value. It will have a section at the bottom of the first page which shows how much lime (if needed) to add for each 1000 square feet and refer you to specific comments on the last page. The comments page will tell you what type of fertilizer you need, how much you need and how to apply it. These recommendations are specific for whatever type of plant you want to grow (as you indicated on the soil test record sheet).

Understanding your Soil Test Report

Soil pH

Soil pH is a measure of how acidic or alkaline your soil is. Soil pH directly affects nutrient availability. The pH scale ranges from 0 to 14, with 7 as neutral. Numbers less than 7 indicate acidity, while numbers greater than 7 indicate an alkaline soil. Plants thrive best in different soil pH ranges. Azaleas, rhododendrons, blueberries and conifers thrive best in acid soils (pH 5.0 to 5.5). Vegetables, grasses and most ornamentals do best in slightly acidic soils (pH 5.8 to 6.5). Soil pH values above or below these ranges may result in less vigorous growth or symptoms of nutrient deficiencies.

Nutrients

Nutrients for healthy plant growth are divided into three categories: primary, secondary and micronutrients. Nitrogen (N), phosphorus (P) and potassium (K) are primary nutrients, which are needed in fairly large quantities compared to the other nutrients. Calcium (Ca), magnesium (Mg) and sulfur (S) are secondary nutrients which are required by the plant in lesser quantities but are no less essential for good plant growth than the primary nutrients. Zinc (Zn) and manganese (Mn) are micronutrients which are required by plants in very small amounts. Most secondary and micronutrient deficiencies are easily corrected by keeping the soil at the optimum pH value.

Nitrogen

Available nitrogen is taken up by plant roots in the form of nitrate and ammonium. Nitrogen testing is not recommended because the levels of available nitrogen are variable due to its mobility in the soil. The available forms of nitrogen are very water soluble and move rapidly through the soil profile with rainfall and irrigation. This causes the amount in the root zone to fluctuate over time. Recommendations are based on the requirements of the particular plants you are growing.

The farmers find it extremely difficult to know the proper type of fertilizer, which would match his soil. In using a fertilizer he must take into account the requirement of his crops and the characteristics of the soil.

The basic objective of the soil-testing programme is to give frmers a service leading to better and more economic use of ertilizers and better soil management practices for increasing agricultura production. High crop yields cannot be obtained withou applying sufficient fertilizers to overcome existing deficiencies.

Efficient use of fertilizers is a major factor in any progrmme designed to bring about an economic increase in agricultural production. The farmers involved in such a programme will hve to use increasing quantities of fertilizers to achieve the desired yield levels. However the amounts and kinds of fertilizers requred for the same crop vary from soil to soil, even field to field on the same soil. The use of fertilizers without first testing the soil is like taking medicine without first consulting a physician to fnd out what is needed. It is observed that the fertilizers increase yields and the farmers are aware of this. But are they applying right quantities of the right kind of fertilizers at the right time at the right place to ensure maximum profit? Without a fertilizer recommendation based upon a soil test, a farmer may be apply use of use of the wrong kinds or amounts, or improper use of fertilisers.

A fertilizers recommendation from a soil testing laboratory is based on carefully conducted soil analyses and the results of up-to-date agronomic research on the crop, and it therefore is most scientific information available for fertilizing that crop in that field.

Each recommendation based on a soil test takes into account the values obtained by these accurate analysis, the research work so far conducted on the crop in the particular soil areas, and the management practices of the concerned farmer. The soil test with the resulting fertilizer recommendation is therefore the actual connecting link between agronomic research and its practical application to the farmers' fields. However, soil testing is not an end in itself. It is a means to an end. A farmer who follows only the soil test recommendations is not assured of a good crop. Good crop yields are the result of the application also of other good management practices, such as proper tillage, efficient water management, good seed, and adequate plant protection measures. Soil testing is essential and is the first step in obtaining high yields and maximum returns from the money invested in fertilizers.

How to Collect a Soil Sample

Sample each field separately. However, where the areas within a field differ distinctly in crop growth, appearance of the soils, or in elevation, or are known to have been cropped or fertilized and manured differently, divided the filed and sample each area separately.

Take a composite sample from each area. Scrape away surface litter, then take a small sample from the surface to plough depth from a number of spots in the field (10 to 15 per acre). Collect these samples in a clean bucket or some such wide container.

Where crops have been planted in lines (rows), sample between the lines.

Do not sample unusual area. Avoid areas recently fertilized, old bunds, marshy spots, near tress, compost piles, other non-representative locations.

Take a uniform thick sample from the surface to plough depth. If a spade or a trowel is used, dig a v-shaped hole, then cut out a uniform thick slice of soil from bottom to op of the exposed soil face, collect the sample on the baled or in your hand and place it in the bucket.

Pour the soil from the bucket on a piece of clean cloth or paper and mix thoroughly, discard, by quartering, all but 1 to 2 lbs. of soil. Quarterly may be done by mixing sample well, dividing it into four equal parts, then rejecting two opposite quarters, mixing the remaining two portions, again dividing into four parts and rejecting two opposite quarters, and so on. The sample should be dried in the shade for an hour or two before it goes into the cloth bag container.

Each cloth bag should be large enough to hold a pound or two of soil, and should be properly marked to identify the sample.

Fill out the soil sample information sheet for each sample. These forms may be sent separately to the laboratory or enclosed with the soil sample.

Address the samples to the Soil Chemist, Soil Testing Laboratory, Goal Ghar, Port Blair.

Keep a record of the areas sampled and a simple sketch map for reference when you get the soil test and fertilizers recommendation report from the soil testing laboratory.

ROLE OF THE EXTENSION SERVICE IN SOIL TESTING

The actual analysis of the sample and the making out of fertilizer recommendation is only part of the soil testing service. To a large measure, the efficiency of this service depends upon the care and effort put froth by extension workers and farmers in the collection and dispatch of samples to the laboratory. Its effectiveness also depends upon the proper follow-through of the fertilizer recommendations, including the establishment of result demonstrations on farmer's fields to induce the farmers to follow the fertilizer recommendations. In this work the staff of the extension service play the most important role, since they are the people directly in contact with the farmers or this reason, the soil chemist in charge of the laboratory must give periodic and through training to the extension staff on these subjects.

A useful soil testing service starts with the collection of representative soil samples. A fertilizer recommendation made after analyzing the soil can only as good as the sample on which it is based. Actually the one to ten grams of soil used for each chemical analysis should represent as accurately as possible the entire surface six inches of soil, weighing about 2 million pounds per acre. The importance of taking a representative composite sample is, therefore, self-evident. One field can be treated as a single sampling unit only if it is relatively uniform and does not exceed approximately five acres. Variations in slope, colour, texture, management, and cropping pattern should be taken into account and separate composite soil sample adequately representing the field, small portions of surface soil should be collected to depth of six inches from at least ten well-distributed spots in the field, mixed well, and about ½ kg of representative sample sent to laboratory.

Proper sampling tools are essential for collection of good soil samples. For a soft. Moist soil, the soil tube, phowda (spade), or khurpi (trowel) are usually quite satisfactory.

For harder soils, a screw type auger, or an adze might be more convenient. Post hole augers are convenient for sampling excessively wet areas like paddy fields. An extension worker whose duties include collection of soil samples should be supplied with at least a few of these tools, and also a plastic bucket. The phowda, khurpi and adze are very common implements available in most hardware shops and so there should be no difficulty in procuring these implements.

The farmers should be given help in filling out the soil sample information sheet with an ex-plantation of any items not understood. It should be remembered that the information sheet is very vital part of procedures that go to make a good soil test recommendation. This sheet must supply all of the background information that, in combination with the results of the analysis, makes possible an accurate fertilizer recommendation for a certain crop, for that particular field. Factors such as crop variety, slope of land, irrigation and drainage facilities, and pervious cropping seasons affect the amounts of fertilizer to be applied to particular crop. Any peculiarities noted in the soil or in the vigor or the crop would be very valuable information on the soil sample information sheet as a basis for making an adequate fertilizer recommendation. In the absence of this information, the soil chemist must base his recommendation upon the soil test values alone, and more often than not the farmer will receive an adequate fertiliser recommendation.

CHAPTER–9

Minerals in Soil

INTRODUCTION

A mineral is a naturally occurring solid formed through geological processes that has a characteristic chemical composition, a highly ordered atomic structure, and specific physical properties. A rock, by comparison, is an aggregate of minerals and need not have a specific chemical composition. Minerals range in composition from pure elements and simple salts to very complex silicates with thousands of known forms. The study of minerals is called mineralogy.

MINERAL DEFINITION AND CLASSIFICATION

To be classified as a true mineral, a substance must be a solid and have a crystalline structure. It must also be a naturally occurring, homogeneous substance with a defined chemical composition. Traditional definitions excluded organically derived material. However, the International Mineralogical Association in 1995 adopted a new definition:

> a mineral is an element or chemical compound that is normally crystalline and that has been formed as a result of geological processes.

The modern classifications include an organic class - in both the new Dana and the Strunz classification schemes.

The chemical composition may vary between end members of a mineral system. For example the plagioclase feldspars comprise a continuous series from sodium-rich albite ($NaAlSi_3O_8$) to calcium-rich anorthite ($CaAl_2Si_2O_8$) with four recognized intermediate compositions between. Mineral-like substances that don't strictly meet the definition are sometimes classified as mineraloids. Other natural-occurring substances are nonminerals. Industrial minerals is a market term and refers to commercially valuable mined materials.

A crystal structure is the orderly geometric spatial arrangement of atoms in the internal structure of a mineral. There are 14 basic crystal lattice arrangements of atoms in three dimensions, and these are referred to as the 14 "Bravais lattices". Each of these lattices can be classified into one of the six crystal systems, and all crystal structures currently recognized fit in one Bravais lattice and one crystal system. This crystal structure is based on regular internal atomic or ionic arrangement that is often expressed in the geometric form that the crystal takes. Even when the mineral grains are too small to see or are irregularly shaped, the underlying crystal structure is always periodic and can be determined by X-ray diffraction. Chemistry and crystal structure together define a mineral. In fact, two or more minerals may have the same chemical composition, but differ in crystal structure (these are known as polymorphs). For example, pyrite and marcasite are both iron sulfide, but their arrangement of atoms differs. Similarly, some minerals have different chemical compositions, but the same crystal structure: for example, halite (made from sodium and chlorine), galena (made from lead and sulfur) and periclase (made from magnesium and oxygen) all share the same cubic crystal structure.

Crystal structure greatly influences a mineral's physical properties. For example, though diamond and graphite have the same composition (both are pure carbon), graphite is very soft, while diamond is the hardest of all known minerals. This happens because the carbon atoms in graphite are arranged into sheets which can slide easily past each other, while the carbon atoms in diamond form a strong, interlocking three-dimensional network.

There are currently more than 4,000 known minerals, according to the International Mineralogical Association, which is responsible for the approval of and naming of new mineral species found in nature. Of these, perhaps 100 can be called "common," 50 are "occasional," and the rest are "rare" to "extremely rare."

DIFFERENCES BETWEEN MINERALS AND ROCKS

A mineral is a naturally occurring solid with a definite chemical composition and a specific crystalline structure. A rock is an aggregate of one or more minerals. (A rock may also include organic remains and mineraloids.) Some rocks are predominantly composed of just one mineral. For example, limestone is a sedimentary rock composed almost entirely of the mineral calcite. Other rocks contain many minerals, and the specific minerals in a rock can vary widely. Some minerals, like quartz, mica or feldspar are common, while others have been found in only four or five locations worldwide. The vast majority of the rocks of the Earth's crust consist of quartz, feldspar, mica, chlorite, kaolin, calcite, epidote, olivine, augite, hornblende, magnetite, hematite, limonite and a few other minerals Over half of the mineral species known are so rare that they have only been found in a handful of samples, and many are known from only one or two small grains.

Commercially valuable minerals and rocks are referred to as industrial minerals. Rocks from which minerals are mined for economic purposes are referred to as ores (the rocks and minerals that remain, after the desired mineral has been separated from the ore, are referred to as tailings).

MINERAL COMPOSITION OF ROCKS

A main determining factor in the formation of minerals in a rock mass is the chemical composition of the mass, for a certain mineral can be formed only when the necessary elements are present in the rock. Calcite is most common in limestones, as these consist essentially of calcium carbonate; quartz is common in sandstones and in certain igneous rocks which contain a high percentage of silica.

Other factors are of equal importance in determining the natural association or paragenesis of rock-forming minerals, principally the mode of origin of the rock and the stages through which it has passed in attaining its present condition. Two rock masses may have very much the same bulk composition and yet consist of entirely different assemblages of minerals. The tendency is always for those compounds to be formed which are stable under the conditions under which the rock mass originated. A granite arises by the consolidation of a molten magma at high temperatures and great pressures and its component minerals are those stable under such conditions. Exposed to moisture, carbonic acid and other subaerial agents at the ordinary temperatures of the Earth's surface, some of these original minerals, such as quartz and white mica are relatively stable and remain unaffected; others weather or decay and are replaced by new combinations. The feldspar passes into kaolinite, muscovite and quartz, and any mafic minerals such as pyroxenes, amphiboles or biotite have been present they are often altered to chlorite, epidote, rutile and other substances. These changes are accompanied by disintegration, and the rock falls into a loose, incoherent, earthy mass which may be regarded as a sand or soil. The materials thus formed may be washed away and deposited as sandstone or siltstone. The structure of the original rock is now replaced by a new one; the mineralogical constitution is profoundly altered; but the bulk chemical composition may not be very different. The sedimentary rock may again undergo metamorphism. If penetrated by igneous rocks it may be recrystallized or, if subjected to enormous pressures with heat and movement during mountain building, it may be converted into a gneiss not very different in mineralogical composition though radically different in structure to the granite which was its original state

PHYSICAL PROPERTIES OF MINERALS

Classifying minerals can range from simple to very difficult. A mineral can be identified by several physical properties, some of them being sufficient for full identification without equivocation. In other cases, minerals can only be classified by more complex chemical or X-ray diffraction analysis; these methods, however, can be costly and time-consuming.

Physical properties commonly used are:

Crystal structure and habit: See the above discussion of crystal structure. A mineral may show good crystal habit or form, or it may be massive, granular or compact with only microscopically visible crystals.

Talc

Rough Diamond Hardness: the physical hardness of a mineral is usually measured according to the Mohs scale. This scale is relative and goes from 1 to 10. Minerals with a given Mohs hardness can scratch the surface of any mineral that has a lower hardness than itself.

Mohs Hardness Scale

1. Talc $Mg_3Si_4O_{10}(OH)_2$
2. Gypsum $CaSO_4{\cdot}2H_2O$
3. Calcite $CaCO_3$
4. Fluorite CaF_2
5. Apaţite $Ca_5(PO_4)_3(OH,Cl,F)$
6. Orthoclase $KAlSi_3O_8$
7. Quartz SiO_2
8. Topaz $Al_2SiO_4(OH,F)_2$
9. Corundum Al_2O_3
10. Diamond C (pure carbon)

Luster indicates the way a mineral's surface interacts with light and can range from dull to glassy (vitreous).

Metallic-high reflectivity like metal: galena and pyrite

Sub-metallic-slightly less than metallic reflectivity: magnetite

Non-metallic Lusters

Adamantine - brilliant, the luster of diamond also cerussite and anglesite.

Vitreous -the luster of a broken glass: quartz.

Pearly - iridescent and pearl-like: talc and apophyllite

Resinous - the luster of resin: sphalerite and sulfur

Silky - a soft light shown by fibrous materials: gypsum and chrysotile

Dull/earthy -shown by finely crystallized minerals: the kidney ore variety of hematite.

Colour indicates the appearance of the mineral in reflected light or transmitted light for translucent minerals (i.e. what it looks like to the naked eye).

Iridescence - the play of colours due to surface or internal interference. Labradorite exhibits internal iridescence whereas hematite and sphalerite often show the surface effect.

Streak refers to the colour of the powder a mineral leaves after rubbing it on an unglazed porcelain streak plate. Note that this is not always the same colour as the original mineral.

Cleavage describes the way a mineral may split apart along various planes. In thin sections, cleavage is visible as thin parallel lines across a mineral.

Fracture describes how a mineral breaks when broken contrary to its natural cleavage planes.

Specific gravity relates the mineral mass to the mass of an equal volume of water, namely the density of the material. While most minerals, including all the common rock-forming minerals, have a specific gravity of 2.5-3.5, a few are noticeably more or less dense, e.g. several sulfide minerals have high specific gravity compared to the common rock-forming minerals.

Other properties: fluorescence (response to ultraviolet light), magnetism, radioactivity, tenacity (response to mechanical induced changes of shape or form), piezoelectricity and reactivity to dilute acids.

CHEMICAL PROPERTIES OF MINERALS

Minerals may be classified according to chemical composition. They are here categorized by anion group. The list below is in approximate order of their abundance in the Earth's crust. The list follows the Dana classification system which closely parallels the Strunz classification.

Silicate Class

The largest group of minerals by far are the silicates (most rocks are = 95% silicates), which are composed largely of silicon and oxygen, with the addition of ions such as aluminium, magnesium, iron, and calcium. Some important rock-forming silicates include the feldspars, quartz, olivines, pyroxenes, amphiboles, garnets, and micas.

Carbonate Class

The carbonate minerals consist of those minerals containing the anion and include calcite and aragonite (both calcium carbonate), dolomite (magnesium/calcium carbonate) and siderite (iron carbonate). Carbonates are commonly deposited in marine settings when the shells of dead planktonic life settle and accumulate on the sea floor. Carbonates are also found in evaporitic settings (e.g. the Great Salt Lake, Utah) and also in karst regions, where the dissolution and reprecipitation of carbonates leads to the formation of caves, stalactites and stalagmites. The carbonate class also includes the nitrate and borate minerals.

Sulfate Class

Sulfates all contain the sulfate anion, $SO4^{2-}$. Sulfates commonly form in evaporitic settings where highly saline waters slowly evaporate, allowing the formation of both sulfates and halides at the water-sediment interface. Sulfates also occur in hydrothermal vein systems as gangue minerals along with sulfide ore minerals. Another occurrence is as secondary oxidation products of original sulfide minerals. Common sulfates include anhydrite (calcium sulfate), celestine (strontium sulfate), barite (barium sulfate), and gypsum (hydrated calcium sulfate). The sulfate class also includes the chromate, molybdate, selenate, sulfite, tellurate, and tungstate minerals.

Halide Class

HaliteThe halides are the group of minerals forming the natural salts and include fluorite (calcium fluoride), halite (sodium chloride), sylvite (potassium chloride), and sal ammoniac (ammonium chloride). Halides, like sulfates, are commonly found in evaporitic settings such as playa lakes and landlocked seas such as the Dead Sea and Great Salt Lake. The halide class includes the fluoride, chloride, bromide and iodide minerals.

Oxide Class

Oxides are extremely important in mining as they form many of the ores from which valuable metals can be extracted. They also carry the best record of changes in the Earth's magnetic field. They commonly occur as precipitates close to the Earth's surface, oxidation products of other minerals in the near surface weathering zone, and as accessory minerals in igneous rocks of the crust and mantle. Common oxides include hematite (iron oxide), magnetite (iron oxide), chromite (iron chromium oxide), spinel (magnesium aluminium oxide - a common component of the mantle), ilmenite (iron titanium oxide), rutile (titanium dioxide), and ice (hydrogen oxide). The oxide class includes the oxide and the hydroxide minerals.

Sulfide Class

Many sulfide minerals are economically important as metal ores. Common sulfides include pyrite (iron sulfide - commonly known as fools' gold), chalcopyrite (copper iron sulfide), pentlandite (nickel iron sulfide), and galena (lead sulfide). The sulfide class also includes the selenides, the tellurides, the arsenides, the antimonides, the bismuthinides, and the sulfosalts (sulfur and a second anion such as arsenic).

Phosphate Class

The phosphate mineral group actually includes any mineral with a tetrahedral unit AO_4 where A can be phosphorus, antimony, arsenic or vanadium. By far the most common phosphate is apatite which is an important biological mineral found in teeth and bones of many animals. The phosphate class includes the phosphate, arsenate, vanadate, and antimonate minerals.

Element Class

The elemental group includes metals and intermetallic elements (gold, silver, copper), semi-metals and non-metals (antimony, bismuth, graphite, sulfur). This group also includes natural alloys, such as electrum (a natural alloy of gold and silver), phosphides, silicides, nitrides and carbides (which are usually only found naturally in a few rare meteorites).

Organic Class

The organic mineral class includes biogenic substances in which geological processes have been a part of the genesis or origin of the existing compound Minerals of the organic class include various oxalates, mellitates, citrates, cyanates, acetates, formates, hydrocarbons and other miscellaneous species Examples include whewellite, moolooite, mellite, fichtelite, carpathite, evenkite and abelsonite.

POTASSIUM IN SOIL

Measurement of soil K availability, as defined by the K^+ potential, has been used extensively by soil scientists for agricultural crops but has had only limited application in environmental studies. The concept of the quantity/potential (Q/P) relationship is applied in tidal floodplain systems to investigate the mineral nutrient K status of contemporary and buried sulfidic/sulfuric soils. Expressed as a ratio of the relative activity and exchange with Ca^{2+} and Mg^{2+}, the K^+ potential is a free energy measure of soil K availability to plants and describes how tightly K is bound to the soil. Results for the acid sulfate soils (ASS) of the South Alligator River floodplain show that the oxidised uppermost soils have decreased equilibrium values of K^+ potential. This contrasted with the sulfidic materials of the subsoil, which exhibited considerably less negative equilibrium K^+ potential values, revealing a significantly greater availability of K. The natural oxidation of sulfide-bearing minerals and sulfuric acid attack on clay minerals during the ripening of ASS, results in changes to the clay mineral structure and depletes K from the clays of the floodplain surface. These pedogenic changes in clay mineralogy are accompanied by natural hydrological and oxidation processes that cause upward leaching and export of K from ASS landscapes. Potassium deficiency is associated with the formation of the sulfide mineral oxidation product jarosite, which acts as an infinite sink for K in the upper sulfuric horizon, and reduces the amount of K that is readily available for plant growth.

Potassium is an essential macronutrient for all plants. Available K includes the K^+ ions in the soil solution and exchangeable K adsorbed on the soil colloid surfaces. The latter form of K^+ is readily released to solution by natural equilibrium processes in the soil, or by exchange when extracted with salt solutions. The concept of a nutrient potential was suggested as a measure of the work a plant must do to remove nutrients from the soil. The classical thermodynamics to soil exchangeable K^+, and Ca_2^+ plus Mg_2^+ release to the soil solution for determining the free energy of K-Ca exchange equilibria in soils. The energy of exchange as a measure of the chemical potential of K in the soil relative to the chemical potential of Ca in the same soil. Subsequently, the difference in free energy between K and divalent ions, such as Ca and Mg, was well correlated with K uptake by ryegrass and could define the K status of soils, provided other soil factors were examined. The ability of a soil to supply K to plants is characterised by both the total amount of nutrient present (quantity, Q) and the energy level at which it is supplied (potential, P). The K^+ potential is a free energy measure of the soil nutrient availability, expressed as a ratio of the relative activity and exchange between K^+ and Ca_2^+ plus Mg_2^+.

Just as the soil moisture characteristic relates the free energy of soil water (i.e. moisture potential) to the amount of water held (i.e. soil moisture content), K^+ potentials are similarly related to the total amount or quantity (Q) of exchangeable K on the soil colloid, and to its removability or intensity (I), measured by Δ GK via the K adsorption curve. Hence, the analogous concept of the moisture characteristic is applied to determine the amount of nutrient available to a plant, called the nutrient capacity of the soil. The nutrient capacity as the ability of a soil to resist change in potential. The soil with the least change in potential for a given change in adsorbed nutrient, in this case K, with minimal slope on the adsorption curve, is referred to as having the greatest capacity for that nutrient. Water soluble K and exchangeable K are readily available to plants and provide most of the available K measured by the K^+ potential, but the availability of K is affected by the supply characteristics of the soil, which influence K^+ uptake. Changes in exchangeable K must be balanced by opposite changes in other exchangeable cations, notably Ca and Mg. The relationship between quantity and potential ("adsorption curves") has commonly been used in agricultural soils to predict K availability to crops, but has had only limited applications in natural vegetation studies under different soil conditions (Jafari 1994). The K^+ potential is a significant means of examining K availability in the stratigraphy of acid sulfate soil (ASS) floodplains and enables some understanding of the morphodynamics, pedogenesis, and vegetation changes in the South Alligator River floodplain during the Holocene.

These sulfidic materials, known as acid sulfate soils, when first deposited from estuarine or brackish water, are often K-rich clays that support widespread mangrove swamps. The large organic inputs from the mangroves, combined with dissolved sulfate and generally reduced conditions, allows the accumulation of sulfide minerals, mainly as cubic iron pyrite. These sulfidic materials oxidise slowly when exposed to air by evapotranspiration under natural conditions (or rapidly with human disturbance such as with excavation or drainage), forming sulfuric acid. At the pedological time scale, the annual export of K in estuaries during the monsoonal wet in northern Australia, depletes K from the ASS of the estuarine floodplain and exports it from the floodplain surface soils to offshore sinks. This paper aims to use K^+ potentials to explain the role of K availability in depositional and oxidation processes in the ASS development of the South Alligator River floodplain.

Methods

Soil Sampling and Profile Descriptions

Soil samples were collected at 0.1 m depth intervals from various depths in ASS profiles on the floodplain of the South Alligator River, Kakadu National Park, in northern Australia. Field descriptions and pH measurements using a hand-held TPS MC-81 pH–Conductivity–Salinity meter were undertaken at these intervals for each soil profile. During collection, precautions were taken to avoid contamination and oxidation prior to transport to the laboratory where the soils were oven-dried at 80-85°C for at least 24 h then passed through a 2 mm sieve in preparation for analysis.

Soil Solution Chemical Analyses

Soil samples were selected for laboratory analysis from various depths in the soil profile, based on horizon or layer differences. Characterisation of the profiles was further made in duplicate with pH measurements in H2O and 1 M KCl extracts (UNICAM 9455 pH/ISE meter), electrical conductivity (EC) measured in H2O extracts (TPS 900-C Conductivity–Salinity meter), and soluble basic cations measured using atomic absorption spectrophotometry (AAS) in H_2O extracts (UNICAM 929 SOLAAR AA spectrometer). All extracts used a 1:5 soil to solution ratio, after the soil had been equilibrated for 0.5 h on an end-over-end shaker. Means and standard errors were calculated for all duplicate extracts.

Soil Solid Phase Chemical Analyses

The distribution of total sulfur in the profile, mainly as the sulfide mineral pyrite, as well as total carbon were determined gravimetrically following dry combustion and analysis of the soil samples by a Leco CNS Analyser. This procedure is based on standard methods of soil analysis, using whole soil samples oven-dried at 60°C and finely ground to <250 μm size fraction.

Mineralogical analyses of the soil samples were determined by x-ray powder diffractometry, and examined on treated oriented aggregate samples of the clay fraction and on an "as received" basis for the identification of clay minerals and mineral phases, respectively. These procedures are based on standard methods of soil analysis, with whole soil samples oven-dried at 60°C and finely ground to 80 μm size fraction.

Results and Discussion

ASS Profile Characteristics

The distribution of the various materials that typify the sedimentary environment of the South Alligator River deltaic-estuarine floodplain. Alluvial floodplain deposits of black organic cracking clays, heavily marked and modified by oxidation, overlie a freshwater-marine transitional zone and blue-grey, estuarine saline mangrove muds at depth. Much of these floodplain soils exhibit a profile form comprised of five distinct soil layers, described as:

1. organic topsoil A horizon;
2. oxidised mottled B layer;
3. transition zone of seasonally oxidised sulfidic materials;
4. reduced sulfidic C layer; and
5. pre-Holocene basal sediments.

Figure 9.1 shows the uppermost four distinct soil layers, which include an organic topsoil A horizon, a clearly defined oxidised and mottled B layer, a seasonally oxidised sulfidic layer and a reduced sulfidic C layer. The seasonally oxidised sulfidic layer, referred to as the transition zone, was of varying thickness and lay between the sulfuric B layer and the underlying sulfidic materials of the C layer. The base of the oxidised zone was generally distinct and the lower limit of oxidation referred to the oxidation front of the soil profile as perceived by the absence of mottles and an increase in pHF values at the base of the transition zone.

The upper and lower floodplain deposits of the South Alligator River were characterised by an organic A horizon as the uppermost soil layer with a matrix colour (moist) of very dark grey (10YR 3/1) in a light medium clay-textured soil containing abundant root material. This layer often had distinct

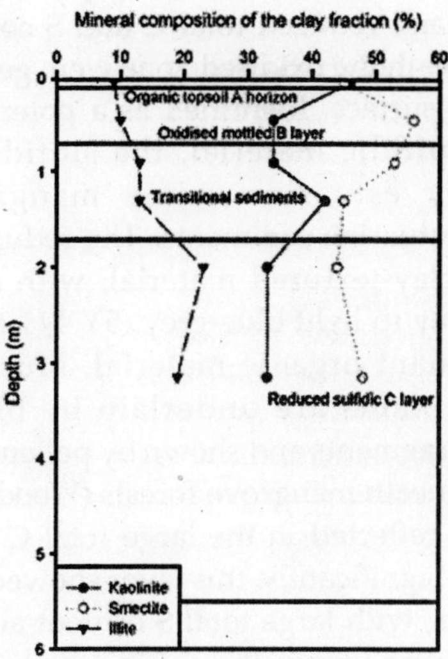

Fig. 9.1: Field pH and total sulfur and carbon contents (g/kg) of a South Alligator River soil profile. Reference lines show the boundary between identified acid sulfate soil layers.

orange mottles (5YR 5/8) of Fe oxides associated with fine roots, large organic matter content evident as total C (Fig. 9.1) and a massive cracking pattern, characteristic of these surface clays. A heavily oxidised and strongly acid B layer of 0.5 to 1 m thick overlay a transitional zone forming a partially oxidised diffuse boundary of similar thickness. The upper 1 to 2 m of the floodplain deposits were described as very dark to dark grey (2.5Y 3/1 to 5Y 4/1) medium clays, with up to 60% pale yellow and orange red mottles of jarosite and Fe oxides, respectively. Identified as an actual acid sulfate soil (AASS) or sulfuric horizon, this layer had a pHF ranging from below 3.70 (mean pHF 4.66) and minimal total S content due to oxidation (Fig. 9.1). The transition zone was a gradational horizon, with a matrix colour (moist) light brownish or olive grey (5Y 6/2) and a medium-heavy clay texture, exhibiting partial oxidation and some reduced components of the subsoil. There was evidence of oxidation, with heavy mottling generally distributed along cracks and relict root channels, concurrent with an increasing pHF from 4.04 to 6.87 (mean pHF 5.44) and reduced total C and S contents (Fig. 9.1). The materials beneath the oxidised zone were generally different from those at the surface. Identified as a potential acid sulfate soil (PASS) or sulfidic material, the sulfidic C layer was characterised by estuarine saline mangrove muds or undifferentiated estuarine sediments. The reduced C layer was typically a silty clay-textured material, with a matrix colour (moist) of dark grey to light blue-grey (5Y 4/1 to 5B 5/1), often containing abundant organic material. Much of the South Alligator River plains are underlain by blue-grey muds containing wood fragments and shown by pollen analysis to have been deposited beneath mangrove forests (Woodroffe et al. 1985, 1986), which was reflected in the large total C contents in this layer (Figure 9.1). Significantly, this layer showed no evidence of oxidation products, with large total S content and no jarosite or Fe mottling occurring within the sulfidic materials and a pHF ranging from 5.25 to 7.35 (mean pHF 6.77)

The results from XRD analysis enabled a general interpretation of the clay mineral composition of the South Alligator River floodplain soils. The dominance of kaolinite in the clays was characteristic of these tropical and weathered acid soils. Figure 9.2 reveals the pattern of decreasing kaolinite from the organic and oxidised surface soils to the transition zone. Below the oxidation front, kaolinite increased in the sulfidic C layer up to 60% of the clay fraction. However, the soils were also characterised by similar amounts of smectite. The presence of expandable 2:1 clay minerals such as smectite reflected the shrink swell nature of the surface Vertosols. Relative amounts of smectite in the clay fraction increased from the organic topsoil to the oxidised B layer and subsequently decreased through the transition zone to the sulfidic C layer for these soils. Illite was a considerably smaller proportion the clay fraction and relatively constant over depth, increasing from around 10% in the organic and oxidised surface soils up to 20% in the sulfidic C layer.

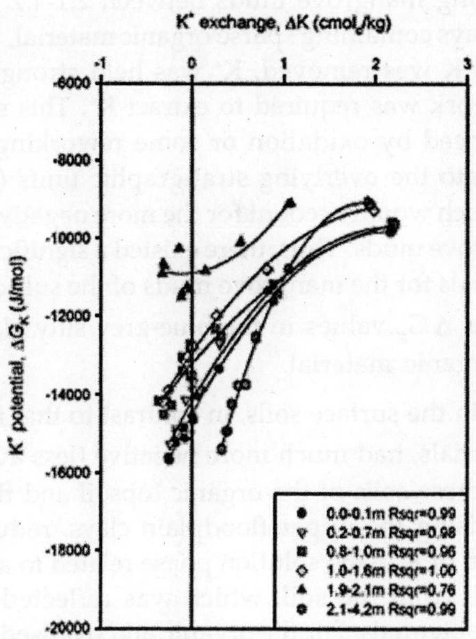

Fig. 9.2: Relationship between K^+ potential and the change in exchangeable K for a South Alligator River floodplain soil profile. The curvilinear lines are regression fits to the data. The vertical reference line shows the equilibrium value of ΔG_K when there is no exchange by K (i.e. Δ K=O).

From Fig. 9.2, the K adsorption curves for sulfidic materials had K at less negative (more available) ΔG_K values. The lack of a distinct Q/I' relationship was evident at 1.9-2.1 m depth, with the regression only accounting for 76% of the variation in ΔG_K. Defined as a mangrove mud, this blue-grey silty clay contained abundant organic material, which probably affected the exchange of K^+ in the soil. The cation exchange for this soil may have been at least in part due to the large amounts of organic matter (see Fig. 9.1). However, this soil had a large capacity for K, as shown by the greater range of ΔK values with minimal change in potential. It was evident that much less work was required in order to remove K+ from this organic silty clay than the underlying mangrove muds between 2.1-4.2 m depth. For these silty clays containing sparse organic material, with potential declining as K was removed, K^+ was held strongly to the clay and more work was required to extract K^+. This soil may have been influenced by oxidation or some reworking of the basal sediments into the overlying stratigraphic units (Woodroffe et al. 1986), which would account for the more negative K^+ potential in the mangrove muds. Thus, there existed a significant difference in K^+ potentials for the mangrove muds of the sulfidic layer, with less negative ΔG_K values in the blue-grey silty clay containing abundant organic material.

The K in the surface soils, in contrast to that in the sulfidic subsoil materials, had much more negative (less available) ΔG_K values. For these soils of the organic topsoil and the oxidised B layer comprising the upper floodplain clays, reductions in the concentration of K in the solution phase related to a lower ability to extract K^+ from the soil, which was reflected in the more negative K^+ potentials. For the organic and oxidised surface soils, the removal of only 0.35 cmolc of K/kg of soil reduced the K^+ potential by 1886 J/mol to –14574 J/mol. By contrast, in the sulfidic material at 2.1-4.2 m depth, the removal of a similar amount at 0.26 cmolc of K/kg caused the K^+ potential to decrease by only 611 J/mol to –11446 J/mol. Therefore, the oxidised surface soils have K held much more strongly and a much reduced ability to supply K to plants. The mangrove muds on the other hand represent a significant K store.

CHAPTER–10

Humic Acid

INTRODUCTION

Humic acid is one of the major components of humic substances which are dark brown and major constituents of soil organic matter humus that contributes to soil chemical and physical quality and are also precursors of some fossil fuels. They can also be found in peat, coal, many upland streams, dystrophic lakes and ocean water.

Humic substances make up a large portion of the dark matter in humus and consist of heterogeneous mixtures of transformed biomolecules exhibiting a supramolecular structure, that can be separated in their small molecular components by sequential chemical fractionation. Since the end of the 18th century, humic substances have been designated as either humic acid, fulvic acid or humin. These fractions are defined strictly on their solubility in either acid or alkali, describing the materials by operation only, thus imparting no chemical information about the extracted materials.

The term 'humic substances' is used in a generic sense to distinguish the naturally occurring material from the chemical extractions named humic acid and fulvic acid, which are defined "operationally" by their solubility in alkali or acid solutions. It is important to note, however, that no sharp divisions exist between humic acids, fulvic acids and humins. They are all part of an extremely heterogeneous supramolecular system and the differences between the subdivisions are due to variations in chemical composition, acidity, degree of hydrophobicity and self-associations of molecules. When humic substances are characterized, especially when functionality is studied, there is always the problem that one usually has to separate the huge number of different bioorganic molecules into homogenous fractions.

Formation of Humic Substances in the Environment

Humic substances arise by the microbial degradation of plant and animal tissues and ultimately biomolecules (lipids, proteins, carbohydrates, lignin) dispersed in the environment after the death of living cells. Humic material is a supramolecular structure of relatively small bio-organic molecules (having molecular mass <1000 Da) self-assembled mainly by weak dispersive forces such as Van der Waals force, p-p, and CH-p bonds into only apparently large molecular sizes (Piccolo, 2002). It is well known that humic substances are the most stable fraction of organic matter in soils and can persist for tens, hundreds or even thousands of years (Stevenson, 1994). Their dark colour is due to quinone structures formed in the oxidative soil conditions which remain trapped in the humic hydrophobic domains.

CHEMICAL CHARACTERISTICS OF HUMIC SUBSTANCES

Recent studies using pyrolysis-FIMS and -GC/MS, multidimensional NMR and synchrotron-based spectroscopy have shown that humic substances posses both aromatic and aliphatic characteristics. The dominant functional groups which contribute to surface charge and reactivity of humic substances are phenolic and carboxylic groups (Stevenson, 1994).

Humic substances may chelate multivalent cations such as Mg^{2+}, Ca^{2+}, and Fe^{2+}. By chelating the ions, they increase the availability of these cations to organisms, including plants.

Determination of Humic Acids in Water Samples

The presence of humic acid in water intended for potable or industrial use can have a significant impact on the treatability of that water and the success of chemical disinfection processes.

Accurate methods of establishing humic acid concentrations are therefore essential in maintaining water supplies, especially from upland peaty catchments in temperate climates.

As a lot of different humic molecules in very diverse physical associations are mixed together in natural environments it is difficult to measure their exact concentrations and allocate them to a certain class of bio-organic molecules. For this reason concentrations of humic acid classes can be estimated out of concentrations of organic matter (typically from concentrations of total organic carbon (TOC) or dissolved organic carbon (DOC).

Extraction procedures are bound to alter some of the chemical linkages present in the soil humic substances (mainly ester bonds in biopolyesters such as cutins and suberins). The humic extracts are composed by large numbers of different bioorganic molecules which have not yet totally separated and identified. However, single classes of biomolecules have been identified in the past by selective extractions and treatments and are represented amino acids, proteins, sugars, fatty acids, resins and waxes.

The International Humic Substances Society (IHSS) has established extraction procedures for humic acid and fulvic acids and provides standard reference materials. The methodology for humic extraction is published by the Soil Science Society of America, Madison, Wisconsin which states that the IHSS method is "a standard method for comparisons between and within laboratories."

ECOLOGICAL EFFECTS

Ray von Wandruszka at the University of Idaho researched the effects of humic substances in water ecology and stated that, "this group of substances is a major part of the humus in soil and water, i.e. the material that results from the decay of organic material and gives the soil its brown colour. Derived from both plant and animal matter, it is widely distributed in natural matrices and has a major influence on their properties. These include the retention of man-made pollutants by soils, and the ability of surface and ground water to transport them. The value of regular additions of organic matter to the soil has been recognized by growers since prehistoric times. However, the chemistry and function of the organic matter have been a subject of controversy since men began their postulating about it in the 18th century. Until the time of Liebig, it was supposed that humus was used directly by plants, but, after Liebig had shown that plant growth depended upon inorganic compounds, many soil scientists held the view that organic matter was useful for fertility only as it was broken down with the release of its constituent nutrient elements into inorganic forms. At the present time most soil scientists hold a more holistic view and at least recognize that humus influences soil fertility through its effect on the water-holding capacity of the soil. Also, since plants have been shown to absorb and translocate the complex organic molecules of systemic insecticides, they can no longer discredit the idea that plants may be able to absorb the soluble forms of humus; this may in fact be an essential process for the uptake of otherwise insoluble iron oxides.

Over the past 150 years much has been learned about the chemistry of organic matter. Some of the earliest work by Sprengel on the fractionation of organic matter still forms the basis of methods currently in use. These methods utilize dilute sodium hydroxide (2 per cent) to separate humus as a colloidal sot from alkali-insoluble plant residues.

From this humus sol, the humic fraction is precipitated by acid which leaves a straw-yellow supernatant, the fulvic fraction. The alcohol soluble portion of the humic fraction is generally named ulmic acid.

Professor Ronald A. Newcomb (SDSU Center for Advanced Water Technologies) researched humates for a patent with his son, Jeremiah Lee Newcomb (Pat. Pend.) on a process for making humates, "various fungi act on lignin in plant residues breaking and recombining the organic compounds into tannins, lignins, ulmic acid, fulvic acid, and so forth. These are the elements in a pond after a heavy leaf fall, and the very reason the algae die during that time."

HUMIC ACID AS A CHELATOR

A substantial fraction of the mass of the humic acids is in carboxylic acid functional groups, which endow these molecules with the ability to chelate (bind) (precipitate in some media, make solution in other media) positively charged multivalent ions (Mg^{2+}, Ca^{2+}, Fe^{2+}, Fe^{3+}, most other "trace elements" of value to plants, as well as other ions that have no positive biological role, such as Cd^{2+} and Pb^{2+}.) This chelation of ions is probably the most important role of humic acids with respect to living systems. By chelating the ions, they facilitate the uptake of these ions by several mechanisms, one of which is preventing their precipitation, another seems to be a direct and positive influence on their bioavailability.

Humus

In soil science, humus refers to any organic matter which has reached a point of stability, where it will break down no further and might, if conditions do not change, remain essentially as it is for centuries, if not millennia.

In agriculture, humus is sometimes also used to describe mature compost, or natural compost extracted from a forest or other spontaneous source for use to amend soil. It is also used to describe a topsoil horizon that contains organic matter (humus type, humus form, humus profile).

Humification

The process of "humification" can occur naturally in soil, or in the production of compost. Chemically stable humus is thought by some to be important to the fertility of soils in both a physical and chemical sense, though some agricultural experts advocate a greater focus on other aspects of nutrient delivery, instead. Physically, it helps the soil retain moisture, and encourages the formation of good soil structure. Chemically, it has many active sites which bind to ions of plant nutrients, making them more available. Humus is often described as the 'life-force' of the soil. Yet it is difficult to define humus in precise terms; it is a highly complex substance, the full nature of which is still not fully understood. Physically, humus can be differentiated from organic matter in that the latter is rough looking material, with coarse plant remains still visible, while once fully humified it becomes more uniform in appearance (a dark, spongy, jelly-like substance) and amorphous in structure. That is, it has no determinate shape, structure or character.

Plant remains (including those that have passed through an animal and are excreted as manure) contain organic compounds: sugars, starches, proteins, carbohydrates, lignins, waxes, resins and organic acids. The process of organic matter decay in the soil begins with the decomposition of sugars and starches from carbohydrates which break down easily as saprotrophs initially invade the dead plant, while the remaining cellulose breaks down more slowly. Proteins decompose into amino acids at a rate depending on carbon to nitrogen ratios. Organic acids break down rapidly, while fats, waxes, resins and lignins remain relatively unchanged for longer periods of time. The humus, that is the end product of this process, is thus a mixture of compounds and complex life chemicals of plant, animal, or microbial origin, which has many functions and benefits in the soil. Earthworm humus (vermicompost) is considered by some to be the best organic manure.

Compost which is readily capable of further decomposition is sometimes referred to as effective or active humus, though again scientists would say that if it is not stable, it's not humus at all. This kind of compost is principally derived from sugars, starches, and proteins, and consists of simple organic (fulvic) acids. It is an excellent source of plant nutrients, but of little value regarding long-term soil structure and tilth. Stable (or passive) humus consisting of humic acids and humins, on the other hand, are so highly insoluble (or tightly bound to clay particles that they cannot be penetrated by microbes) that they are greatly resistant to further decomposition. Thus they add few readily available nutrients to the soil, but play an essential part in providing its physical structure. Some very stable humus complexes have survived for thousands of years. Stable humus tends to originate from woodier plant materials, eg, cellulose and lignins. Soil animals, which ingest then transform organic matter in their guts, are active agents of humification, in association with fungi and bacteria: most humus in the soil is included in animal feces of more or less dark colour according to their content in organic matter.

Benefits of Humus

The mineralization process that converts raw organic matter to the relatively stable substance that is humus feeds the soil population of micro-organisms and other creatures, thus maintaining high and healthy levels of soil life.

The rate at which raw organic matter is converted into humus promotes (when fast) or limits (when slow) the coexistence of plants, animals and microbes in terrestrial ecosystems.

Effective and stable humus (see below) are further sources of nutrients to microbes, the former providing a readily available supply while the latter acts as a more long-term storage reservouir.

Humification of dead plant material causes complex organic compounds to break down into simpler forms which are then made available to growing plants for uptake through their root systems.

Humus is a colloidal substance, and increases the soil's cation exchange capacity, hence its ability to store nutrients by chelation as can clay particles; thus while these nutrient cations are accessible to plants, they are held in the soil safe from leaching away by rain or irrigation.

Humus can hold the equivalent of 80-90% of its weight in moisture, and therefore increases the soil's capacity to withstand drought conditions.

The biochemical structure of humus enables it to moderate—or buffer—excessive acid or alkaline soil conditions.

During the humification process, microbes secrete sticky gums; these contribute to the crumb structure of the soil by holding particles together, allowing greater aeration of the soil. Toxic substances such as heavy metals, as well as excess nutrients, can be chelated (that is, bound to the complex organic molecules of humus) and prevented from entering the wider ecosystem.

The dark colour of humus (usually black or dark brown) helps to warm up cold soils in the spring.

CHAPTER–11

Soil Science

INTRODUCTION

Soil science is the study of soil as a natural resource on the surface of the earth including soil formation, classification and mapping; physical, chemical, biological, and fertility properties of soils; and these properties in relation to the use and management of soils.

Sometimes terms which refer to branches of soil science, such as pedology (formation, chemistry, morphology and classification of soil) and edaphology (influence of soil on organisms, especially plants), are used as if synonymous with soil science. The diversity of names associated with this discipline is related to the various associations concerned. Indeed, engineers, agronomists, chemists, geologists, geographers, biologists, microbiologists, sylviculturists, sanitarians, archaeologists, and specialists in regional planning, all contribute to further knowledge of soils and the advancement of the soil sciences.

Fields of Study

Soil occupies the pedosphere, one of Earth's spheres that the geosciences use to organize the Earth conceptually. This is the conceptual perspective of pedology and edaphology, the two main branches of soil science. Pedology is the study of soil in its natural setting. Edaphology is the study of soil in relation to soil-dependent uses. Both branches apply a combination of soil physics, soil chemistry, and soil biology. Due to the numerous interactions between the biosphere, atmosphere and hydrosphere that are hosted within the pedosphere, more integrated, less soil-centric concepts are also valuable. Many concepts essential to understanding soil come from individuals not identifiable strictly as soil scientists. This highlights the interdisciplinary nature of soil concepts.

Research

Dependence on and curiosity about soil, exploring the diversity and dynamic of this resource continues to yield fresh discoveries and insights. New avenues of soil research are compelled by a need to understand soil in the context of climate change greenhouse gases and carbon sequestration. Interest in maintaining the planet's biodiversity and in exploring past cultures has also stimulated renewed interest in achieving a more refined understanding of soil.

Mapping

Most knowledge of soil in nature comes from soil survey efforts. Soil survey, or soil mapping, is the process of determining the soil types or other properties of the soil cover over a landscape, and mapping them for others to understand and use. It relies heavily on distinguishing the individual influences of the five classic soil forming factors. This effort draws upon geomorphology, physical geography, and analysis of vegetation and land-use patterns. Primary data for the soil survey are acquired by field sampling and supported by remote sensing.

Classification

The WRB borrows from modern soil classification concepts, including USDA soil taxonomy. The classification is based mainly on soil morphology as an expression pedogenesis. A major difference with USDA soil taxonomy is that soil climate is not part of the system, except insofar as climate influences soil profile characteristics.

Many other classification schemes exist, including vernacular systems. The structure in vernacular systems are either nominal, giving unique names to soils or landscapes, or descriptive, naming soils by their characteristics such as red, hot, fat, or sandy. Soils are distinguished by obvious characteristics, such as physical appearance (e.g., colour, texture, landscape position), performance (e.g., production capability, flooding), and accompanying vegetation. A vernacular distinction familiar to many is classifying texture as heavy or light. Light soil content and better structure, take less effort to turn and cultivate. Contrary to popular belief light soils do not weigh less than heavy soils on an air dry basis nor do they have more porosity.

History

Vasily Dokuchaev, a Russian geologist, geographer and early soil scientist, is credited with identifying soil as a resource whose distinctness and complexity deserved to be separated conceptually from geology and crop production and treated as a whole.

Previously, soil had been considered a product of chemical transformations of rocks, a dead substrate from which plants derive nutritious elements. Soil and bedrock were in fact equated. Dokuchaev considers the soil as a natural body having its own genesis and its own history of development, a body with complex and multiform processes taking place within it. The soil is considered as different from bedrock. The latter becomes soil under the influence of a series of soil-formation factors (climate, vegetation, country, relief and age). According to him, soil should be called the "daily" or outward horizons of rocks regardless of the type; they are changed naturally by the common effect of water, air and various kinds of living and dead organisms.

A 1914 encyclopedic definition: "the different forms of earth on the surface of the rocks, formed by the breaking down or weathering of rocks"serves to illustrate the historic view of soil which persisted from the 19th century. Dokuchaev's late 19th century soil concept developed in the 20th century to one of soil as earthy material that has been altered by living processes A corollary concept is that soil without a living component is simply a part of earth's outer layer.

Further refinement of the soil concept is occurring in view of an appreciation of energy transport and transformation within soil. The term is popularly applied to the material on the surface of the earth's moon and Mars, a usage acceptable within a portion of the scientific community. Accurate to this modern understanding of soil is Nikiforoff's 1959 definition of soil as the "excited skin of the sub aerial part of the earth's crust".

AREAS OF PRACTICE

Academically, soil scientists tend to be drawn to one of five areas of specialization: microbiology, pedology, edaphology, physics or chemistry. Yet the work specifics are very much dictated by the challenges facing our civilization's desire to sustain the land that supports it, and the distinctions between the sub-disciplines of soil science often blur in the process. Soil science professionals commonly stay current in soil chemistry, soil physics, soil microbiology, pedology, and applied soil science in related disciplines.

One interesting effort drawing in soil scientists in the USA as of 2004 is the Soil Quality Initiative. Central to the Soil Quality Initiative is developing indices of soil health and then monitoring them in a way that gives us long term (decade-to-decade) feedback on our performance as stewards of the planet. The effort includes understanding the functions of soil microbiotic crusts and exploring the potential to sequester atmospheric carbon in soil organic matter. The concept of soil quality, however, has not been without its share of controversy and criticism, including critiques by Nobel Laureate Norman Borlaug and World Food Prize Winner Pedro Sanchez.

A more traditional role for soil scientists has been to map soils. Most every area in the United States now has a published soil survey, which includes interpretive tables as to how soil properties support or limit activities and uses. An internationally accepted soil taxonomy allows uniform communication of soil characteristics and functions. National and international soil survey efforts have given the profession unique insights into landscape scale functions.

BIOMASS

Biomass, as a renewable energy source, refers to living and recently dead biological material that can be used as fuel or for industrial production. In this context, biomass refers to plant matter grown to generate electricity or produce biofuel, and it also includes plant or animal matter used for production of fibers, chemicals or heat. Biomass may also include biodegradable wastes that can be burnt as fuel. It excludes organic material which has been transformed by geological processes into substances such as coal or petroleum.

Industrial biomass can be grown from numerous types of plants, including miscanthus, switchgrass, hemp, corn, poplar, willow, sorghum, sugarcane and a variety of tree species, ranging from eucalyptus to oil palm (palm oil). The particular plant used is usually not very important to the end products, but it does affect the processing of the raw material. Production of biomass is a growing industry as interest in sustainable fuel sources is growing.

Although fossil fuels have their origin in ancient biomass, they are not considered biomass by the generally accepted definition because they contain carbon that has been "out" of the carbon cycle for a very long time. Their combustion therefore disturbs the carbon dioxide content in the atmosphere.

Plastics from biomass, like some recently developed to dissolve in seawater, are made the same way as petroleum-based plastics, are actually cheaper to manufacture and meet or exceed most performance standards. But they lack the same water resistance or longevity as conventional plastics.

ENVIRONMENTAL IMPACT

Biomass is part of the carbon cycle. Carbon from the atmosphere is converted into biological matter by photosynthesis. On death or combustion the carbon goes back into the atmosphere as carbon dioxide (CO_2). This happens over a relatively short timescale and plant matter used as a fuel can be constantly replaced by planting for new growth. Therefore a reasonably stable level of atmospheric carbon results from its use as a fuel. It is accepted that the amount of carbon stored in dry wood is approximately 50% by weight.

Though biomass is a renewable fuel, and is sometimes called a "carbon neutral" fuel, its use can still contribute to global warming. This happens when the natural carbon equilibrium is disturbed; for example by deforestation or urbanization of green sites. When biomass is used as a fuel, as a replacement for fossil fuels, it still puts the same amount of CO_2 into the atmosphere. However, when biomass is used for energy production it is widely considered carbon neutral, or a net reducer of greenhouse gasses because of the offset of methane that would have otherwise entered the atmosphere. The carbon in biomass material, which makes up approximately fifty percent of its dry-matter content, is already part of the atmospheric carbon cycle. Biomass absorbs CO_2 from the atmosphere during its growing lifetime, after which its carbon reverts to the atmosphere as a mixture of CO_2 and methane (CH_4), depending on the ultimate fate of the biomass material. CH_4 converts to CO_2 in the atmosphere, completing the cycle. In contrast to biomass carbon, the car from long-term storage, and adds it to the stock of carbon in the atmospheric cycle.

Energy produced from biomass residues displaces the production of an equivalent amount of energy from fossil fuels, leaving the fossil carbon in storage. It also shifts the composition of the recycled carbon emissions associated with the disposal of the biomass residues from a mixture of CO_2 and CH_4, to almost exclusively CO_2. In the absence of energy production applications, biomass residue carbon would be recycled to the atmosphere through some combination of rotting (biodegradation) and open burning. Rotting produces a mixture of up to fifty percent CH_4, while open burning produces five to ten percent CH_4. Controlled combustion in a power plant converts virtually all of the carbon in the biomass to CO_2. Because CH_4 is a much stronger greenhouse gas than CO_2, shifting CH_4 emissions to CO_2 by converting biomass residues to energy significantly reduces the greenhouse warming potential of the recycled carbon associated with other fates or disposal of the biomass residues.

The existing commercial biomass power generating industry in the United States, which consists of approximately 1,700 MW (megaatts) of operating capacity actively supplying power to the grid, poduces about 0.5 per cent of the U.S. electricity supply. Thi level of biomass power generation avoids approximately 11 million ons per year of CO_2 emissions from fossil fuel combustion. It also avoids approximately two million tons per year of CH_4 emissions from the biomass residues that, in the absence of energy production, would otherwise be disposed of by burial (in landfills,in disposal piles, or by the plowing under of agricultural resides), by spreading, and by open burning. The avoided CH_4 emisions associated with biomass energy production have a greenhouse warming potential that is more than 20 times greater than that of the avoided fossil-fuel CO_2 emissions. Biomass powerproduction is at least five times more effective in reducing greenhouse gas emissions than any other greenhouse-gas-neutral power-production technology, such as other renewable and nuclear.

Currently, the New Hope Power Partnership, is the largest biomass pwer plant in North America. The 140 MWH facility uses sugar cane fiber (bagasse) and recycled urban wood as fuel to generate enough power for its large milling and refining operations as ell as to supply renewable electricity for nearly 60,000 homes. The facility reduces dependence on oil by more than one million barrels per year, and by recycling sugar cane and wood waste, preserves landfill space in urban communities in Florida. Anyways, most of the time the amount of biomass available is not as big as stated in the example above. Many times, especially in Europe where such huge agricultural developments like in the USA are not usual, the cost for transporting the biomass overcomes its actual value and therefore the gathering ground has to be limited to a certain small area. This fact leads to only small possible power outputs around 1 MWel. To make an economic operation possible those power plants have to be equipped with the ORC technology, a cycle similar to the water steam power process just with an organic working medium. Such small power plants can be found in Europe.

Despite harvesting, biomass crops may sequester (trap) carbon. So for example soil organic carbon has been observed to be greater in switchgrass stands than in cultivated cropland soil, especially at depths below 12 inches. The grass sequesters the carbon in its increased root biomass. But the perennial grass may need to be allowed to grow for several years before increases are measurable.[Such small power plants can be found in Europe.

There are several nutrients that are essential for plant growth. A soil test is used to determine the amount of these nutrients in the soil. The soil test results are subsequently used to make a soil test report. In addition to indicating the level of nutrients in your soil, the report will also tell you the pH value or how acidic or basic your soil is, and it will make a recommendation for the amount and type of fertilizer and/or lime you need to add to the soil for optimum plant growth. This allows you to customize your soil fertilizer and lime applications to your plants' needs. Following the recommendations will help prevent problems with nutrient deficiencies (in the case of under-fertilization) or problems associated with over-fertilization such as excessive vegetative growth, delayed maturity, salt burn and wasted money. In addition, it can protect against any environmental hazards resulting from excessive fertilizer applications.

HOW TO TAKE SOIL SAMPLES

To have a soil analysis done you need to collect 12 or more cores which will be combined as one composite sample. The samples should include soil from the surface to a depth of 6 inches in all areas except for lawns where cores should be taken from a depth of only 2 to 3 inches. A simple garden trowel can be used to collect the samples. Place the samples in a clean bucket and mix them thoroughly. It is imperative to use clean sampling tools. Pesticide or fertilizer residues will create misleading results. The sample must not be excessively wet before it goes to the lab. Bring a minimum of 2 cups of soil per sample to your county Extension office. Be sure to keep track of which part of your yard the sample came from. At the Extension office they will ask you to fill out the information on a soil test box, fill out a record sheet and check the appropriate boxes for the analyses desired. The cost of a standard soil test is $6.00 per sample. This test provides unbiased, scientific information on:

- The soil pH value.
- The current soil levels of phosphorus, potassium, calcium, magnesium, zinc and manganese.
- Fertilizer and lime recommendations (if needed) for the plants you are growing.

How Many Samples to Take

You need to take a soil sample from each section of your yard or garden. Usually this means, for example, one sample in your turf area, one in any foundation or perennial bed and one in your vegetable garden. If you have a problem area where plants do not seem to grow well, take a separate soil sample from that location.

Sampling Frequency

The Clemson University Extension Service recommends soil sampling every year.

Time of Sampling

Soil samples can be taken at any time of the year, but it is best to sample the soil a couple months before planting a garden, establishing perennials or before the optimum time for fertilizing lawns to allow ample time for the lime to react with the soil.

Soil Test Results

Within seven to fourteen days, a copy of your soil analysis will be mailed directly to you from the Agricultural Service Lab. Your county Extension office will also receive a copy. Your soil analysis will have a bar graph representing the amount of soil nutrients found and the soil pH value. It will have a section at the bottom of the first page which shows how much lime (if needed) to add for each 1000 square feet and refer you to specific comments on the last page. The comments page will tell you what type of fertilizer you need, how much you need and how to apply it. These recommendations are specific for whatever type of plant you want to grow (as you indicated on the soil test record sheet).

Understanding your Soil Test Report

Soil pH

Soil pH is a measure of how acidic or alkaline your soil is. Soil pH directly affects nutrient availability. The pH scale ranges from 0 to 14, with 7 as neutral. Numbers less than 7 indicate acidity, while numbers greater than 7 indicate an alkaline soil. Plants thrive best in different soil pH ranges. Azaleas, rhododendrons, blueberries and conifers thrive best in acid soils (pH 5.0 to 5.5). Vegetables, grasses and most ornamentals do best in slightly acidic soils (pH 5.8 to 6.5). Soil pH values above or below these ranges may result in less vigorous growth or symptoms of nutrient deficiencies.

Nutrients

Nutrients for healthy plant growth are divided into three categories: primary, secondary and micronutrients. Nitrogen (N), phosphorus (P) and potassium (K) are primary nutrients, which are needed in fairly large quantities compared to the other nutrients. Calcium (Ca), magnesium (Mg) and sulfur (S) are secondary nutrients which are required by the plant in lesser quantities but are no less essential for good plant growth than the primary nutrients. Zinc (Zn) and manganese (Mn) are micronutrients which are required by plants in very small amounts. Most secondary and micronutrient deficiencies are easily corrected by keeping the soil at the optimum pH value.

Nitrogen

Available nitrogen is taken up by plant roots in the form of nitrate and ammonium. Nitrogen testing is not recommended because the levels of available nitrogen are variable due to its mobility in the soil. The available forms of nitrogen are very water soluble and move rapidly through the soil profile with rainfall and irrigation. This causes the amount in the root zone to fluctuate over time. Recommendations are based on the requirements of the particular plants you are growing.

CHAPTER–12

Soil Salinity

INTRODUCTION

Soil salinity is the salt content in the soil.

Salt affected soils are caused by excess accumulation of salts, typically most pronounced at the soil surface. Salts can be transported to the soil surface by capillary transport from a salt laden water table and then accumulate due to evaporation; they can also be concentrated in soils due to human activity. As soil salinity increases, salt effects can result in degradation of soils and vegetation.

Salinization is a process that results from:

- high levels of salt in the soils;
- landscape features that allow salts to become mobile (movement of water table);
- climatic trends that favor accumulation;
- human activities such as land clearing and aquaculture activities.

Salt is a natural element of soils and water. The ions responsible for salinization are: Na^{+}, K^{+}, Ca^{2+}, Mg^{2+} and Cl^{-}.

As the Na^{+} (sodium) predominates, soils can become sodic. Sodic soils present particular challenges because they tend to have very poor structure which limits or prevents water infiltration and drainage.

Over eons, as soil minerals weather and release salts, these salts are flushed or leached out of the soil by drainage water in areas with sufficient precipitation. In addition to mineral weathering, salts are also deposited via dust and precipitation. In dry regions salts may accumulate, leading to naturally saline soils. This is the case, for example, in large parts of Australia. Human practices can increase the salinity of soils by the addition of salts in irrigation water. Proper irrigation management can prevent salt accumulation by providing adequate drainage water to leach added salts from the soil. Disrupting drainage patterns that provide leaching can also result in salt accumulations. An example of this occurred in Egypt in 1970 when the Aswan High Dam was built. The change in the level of ground water before the construction had enabled soil erosion, which led to high concentration of salts in the water table. After the construction, the continuous high level of the water table led to the salination of the arable land.

Salinity from drylands can occur when the water table is between two to three metres from the surface of the soil. The salts from the groundwater are raised by capillary action to the surface of the soil. This occurs when groundwater is saline (which is true in many areas), and is favoured by land use practices allowing more rainwater to enter the aquifer than it could accommodate. For example, the clearing of trees for agriculture is a major reason for dryland salinity in some areas, since deep rooting of trees has been replaced by shallow rooting of annual crops.

Salinity from irrigation can occur over time wherever irrigation occurs, since almost all water (even natural rainfall) contains some dissolved salts. When the plants use the water, the salts are left behind in the soil and eventually begin to accumulate. Since soil salinity makes it more difficult for plants to absorb soil moisture, these salts must be leached out of the plant root zone by applying additional water. This water in excess of plant needs is called the leaching fraction. Salination from irrigation water is also greatly increased by poor drainage and use of saline water for irrigating agricultural crops.

Salinity in urban areas often results from the combination of irrigation and groundwater processes. Irrigation is also now common in cities (gardens and recreation areas).

The consequences of salinity are:

- detrimental effects on plant growth and yield;
- damage to infrastructure (roads, bricks, corrosion of pipes and cables);
- reduction of water quality for users, sedimentation problems;
- soil erosion ultimately, when crops are too strongly affected by the amounts of salts.

Salinity is an important land degradation problem. Soil salinity can be reduced by leaching soluble salts out of soil with excess irrigation water. High levels of soil salinity can be tolerated if salt-tolerant plants are grown.

From the FAO/UNESCO Soil Map of the World the following salinised areas can be derived.

Soil Acidification

Soil acidification is the buildup of hydrogen cations, also called protons, in the soil. This happens when a proton donor is added to the soil. The donor can be an acid, such as nitric acid and sulfuric acid (these acids are common components of acid rain). It can also be a compound such as aluminium sulfate, which reacts in the soil to release protons. Many nitrogen compounds, which are added as fertilizer, also acidify soil over the long term because they produce the ammonium ion which is a proton donor.

Acidification also occurs when base cations such as calcium, magnesium, potassium and sodium are lost from the soil. Losses occur when these bases are leached from the soil. This leaching increases with increasing precipitation. Acid rain accelerates the leaching of bases. Plants take bases from the soil as they grow, donating a proton in exchange for each base cation. Where plant material is removed, as when a forest is logged or crops are harvested, the bases they have taken up are permanently lost from the soil.

Many plants produce organic acids. Where plant litter accumulates on or is incorporated to the soil, these acids (including acetic acid, humic acid, (oxalic acid, and tannic acid) are liberated. This is especially acute in soils under coniferous trees such as pine, spruce and fir, which return fewer base cations to the soil than do most deciduous trees. Certain parent materials also contribute to soil acidification. Granites and their allied igneous rocks are called "acidic" because they have a lot of free quartz, which produces silicic acid on weathering. Also, they have relatively low amounts of calcium and magnesium. Some sedimentary rocks such as shale and coal are rich in sulfides, which, when hydrated and oxidized, produce sulfuric acid which is much stronger than silicic acid. Many coal spoils are too acidic to support vigorous plant growth, and coal gives off strong precursors to acid rain when it is burned. Marine clays are also sulfide-rich in many cases, and such clays become very acidic if they are drained to an oxidizing state.

Acidification may also occur from nitrogen emissions into the air, as the nitrogen may end up deposited into the soil.

Some chemicals which acidify the soil:

- Aluminium sulfate.
- Ammonia.
- Ammonium nitrate.
- Ammonium phosphate.
- Ammonium sulfate.
- Ferrous sulfate.
- Monopotassium phosphate.
- Phosphoric acid.
- Urea.
- Urea phosphate.

Salinity Control

Salinity control relates to controlling the problem of soil salinity and reclaiming salinized agricultural land.

The aim of soil salinity control is to prevent soil degradation by salinization and reclaim already salty (saline) soils. Soil reclamation is also called soil improvement, rehabilitation, remediation, recuperation, or amelioration.

THE SOIL SALINITY PROBLEM

Salty (saline) soils are soils that have a high salt content. The predominant salt is normally sodium chloride (NaCl, "table salt"). Saline soils are therefore also sodic soils but there may be sodic soils that are not saline but alkaline.

Salty soils are a common feature in irrigated lands in arid and semi-arid regions as well as areas that have poor or little crop production. The problems are often associated with high water tables, caused by a lack of natural subsurface drainage to the underground. Poor subsurface drainage may be caused by insufficient transport capacity of the aquifer or because water cannot exit the aquifer for instance, if it is situated in a topographical depression.

Worldwide, the major factor in the development of saline soils is a lack of precipitation. Most naturally saline soils are found in (semi)arid regions and climates of the globe.

The prime cause of human-caused salinization is irrigation. River water used in irrigation contains salts. All irrigation water, however 'sweet', contains salts that remain behind in the soil after the water has evaporated.

For example, assuming irrigation water with a low salt concentration of 0.3 g/l (equal to 0.3 kg/m^3 corresponding to an electric conductivity of about 0.5 dS/m) and a modest annual supply of irrigation water of 10,000 m^3/ha (almost 3 mm/day) brings 3,000 kg salt/ha each year. In the absence of sufficient natural drainage (as in waterlogged soils) and without a proper leaching and drainage program to remove salts, this would lead to a high soil salinity and reduced crop yields in the long run.

Much of the water used in irrigation has a higher salt content than in this example, which is compounded by that fact that many irrigation projects use a far greater annual supply of water. Sugar cane, for example, needs about 20000 m3/ha of water per year. As a result, irrigated areas often receive more than 3,000 kg/ha of salt per year and some receive as much as 10,000 kg/ha/year.

The secondary cause of salinzation is that irrigation can cause a rise in the water table which can prevents salts in irrigated water from dispersing. Irrigation causes enormous changes to the natural water balance of irrigated lands. Large quantities of water in irrigation projects are not consumed by plants and must go somewhere. In irrigation projects it is impossible to achieve 100% irrigation efficiency where all the irrigation water is consumed by the plants. The maximum attainable irrigation efficiency is about 70% but usually it is less than 60%. This means that minimum 30%, but usually more than 40% of the irrigation water is not evaporated and it must go somewhere.

Most of the water lost this way is stored underground which can change the original hydrology of local aquifers considerably. Many aquifers cannot absorb these quantities of water and, the water table rises leading to waterlogging.

Water logging causes two problems: it reduces the yield of most crops and leads to an accumulation of salts brought in with the irrigation water.

Normally, the salinization of agricultural land affects a considerable area of irrigation projects, on the order of 20 to 30%. When the agriculture in such a fraction of the land is abandoned, a new salt and water balance is attained, a new equilibrium is reached, and the situation becomes stable.

In India alone, thousands of square kilometers have been severely salinized. China and Pakistan do not lag much behind (perhaps China has even more salt affected land than India). A regional distribution of the 3,230,000 km² of saline land world wide is shown in the following table derived from the FAO/ UNESCO Soil Map of the World

Although the principles of the processes of salinization are fairly easy to understand, it is more difficult to explain why certain parts of the land suffer from the problems and other parts do not, or to predict accurately which part of the land will fall victim. The main reason for this is the variation of natural conditions in time and space, the usually uneven distribution of the irrigation water, and the seasonal or yearly changes of agricultural practices.

Only in lands with undulating topography the explanation and prediction is pretty simple: the depression areas will degrade the most. The preparation of salt and water balances for distinguishable sub-areas in the irrigation project, or the use of agro-hydro-salinity models can be helpful in explaining or predicting the extent and severity of the problems.

PRINCIPLES OF SALINITY CONTROL

Drainage is the primary method of controlling soil salinity. The system should permit a small fraction of the irrigation water (about 10 to 20 per cent, the drainage or leaching fraction) to be drained and discharged out of the irrigation project.

In irrigated areas where salinity is stable, the salt concentration of the drainage water is normally 5 to 10 times higher than that of the irrigation water. Salt export matches salt import and salt will not accumulate.

When reclaiming already salinized soils, the salt concentration of the drainage water will initially be much higher than that of the irrigation water (for example 50 times higher). Salt export will greatly exceed salt import, so that with the same drainage fraction a rapid desalinization occurs. After one or two years, the soil salinity is decreased so much, that the salinity of the drainage water has come down to a normal value and a new, favorable, equilibrium is reached.

In regions with pronounced dry and wet seasons, drainage may be operated to the wet season, and closed during the dry season. This practice of checked drainage saves irrigation water.

The discharge of salty drainage water problem may pose environmental problems to downstream areas. The environmental hazards must be considered very carefully and, if necessary mitigating measures must be taken. If possible, the drainage must be limited to wet seasons only, when the salty effluent does inflict the least harm. The environmental issues will not be further discussed here.

Drainage Systems

Parameters of a Horizontal Drainage System

Parameters of a vertical drainage systemLand drainage for soil salinty control is usually by horizontal drainage system (figure left), but vertical systems (figure right) are also employed.

The drainage system designed to evacuate salty water also lowers the water table. To reduce the cost of the system, the lowering must be reduced to a minimum. The highest permissible level of the water table (or the shallowest permissible depth) depends on the irrigation and agricultural practices and kind of crops.

In many cases a seasonal average water table depth of 0.6 to 0.8 m is deep enough. This means that the water table may occasionally be less than 0.6 m (say 0.2 m just after an irrigation or a rain storm). This automatically implies that, in other occasions, the water table will be deeper than 0.8 m (say 1.2 m). The fluctuation of the water table helps in the breathing function of the soil while the expulsion of carbon dioxide (CO_2) produced by the plant roots and the inhalation of fresh oxygen (O_2) is promoted.

The establishing of a not too deep water table offers the additional advantage that excessive field irrigation is discouraged, as the crop yield would be negatively affected by the resulting elevated water table, and irrigation water may be saved.

The statements made above on the optimum depth of the watertable are very general, because in some instances the required water table may be still shallower than indicated (for example in rice paddies), while in other instances it must be considerably deeper (for example in some orchards). The establishment of the optimum depth of the water table is in the realm of agricultural drainage criteria.

SOIL LEACHING

The unsaturated zone or vadose zone of the soil below the soil surface and the watertable is subject to four main hydrological inflow and outflow factors:

- Infiltration of rain and irrigation water (Irr) into the soil through the soil surface (Inf): Inf = Rain + Irr.
- Evaporation of soil water through plants and directly into the air through the soil surface (Evap).
- Percolation of water from the unsaturated zone soil into the groundwater through the watertable (Perc).
- Capillary rise of groundwater moving by capillary suction forces into the unsaturated zone (Cap).

In steady state (i.e. the amount of water stored in the unsaturated zone does not change in the long run) the water balance of the unsaturated zone reads: Inflow = Outflow, thus:

Inf + Cap = Evap + Perc or: Irr + Rain + Cap = Evap + Perc

and the salt balance is

$Irr.C_i + Cap.C_c = Evap.F_c.C_e + Perc.C_p + S_s$

where C_i is the salt concentration of the irrigation water, Cc is the salt concentration of the capillary rise, equal to the salt concentration of the upper part of the groundwater body, F_c is the fraction of the total evaporation transpired by plants, C_e is the salt concentration of the water taken up by the plant roots, C_p is the salt concentration of the percolation water, and S_s is the increase of salt storage in the unsaturated soil. This assumes that the rainfall contains no salts. Only along the coast this may not be true. Further it is assumed that no runoff or surface drainage occurs.

The amount of salts removed by plants ($Evap.F_c.C_e$) is usually negligibly small: $Evap.F_c.C_e = 0$

Leaching curves, calibrating leaching efficiencyThe salt concentration C_p can be taken as a part of the salt concentration of the soil in the unsaturated zone (C_u) giving: $C_p = L_e.C_u$, where L_e is the leaching efficiency. The leaching efficiency is often in the order of 0.7 to 0.8, but in poorly structured, heavy clay soils it may be less. In the Leziria Grande polder in the delta of the Tagus river in Portugal it was found that the leaching efficiency was only 0.15.

Assuming that one wishes to avoid the soil salinity to increase and maintain the soil salinity C_u at a desired level C_d we have:

$Ss = 0$, $C_u = C_d$ and $C_p = L_e.C_d$. Hence the salt balance can be simplified to:

$$Perc.L_e.C_d = Irr.C_i + Cap.C_c$$

Setting the amount percolation water required to fulfill this salt bala equal to Lr (the leaching requirement) it is found that:

$$Lr = (Irr.C_i + Cap.C_c)/L_e.C_d.$$

Substituting herein Irr = Evap + Perc - Rain - Cap and re-arranging gives:

$$L_r = [\ (Evap\text{-}Rain).C_i + Cap(C_c\text{-}C_i)\ ]/(L_e.C_d - C_i)$$

With this the irrigation and drainage requirements for salinity control can can be computed too.

In irrigation projects in (semi)arid zones and climates it is important to check the leaching requirement, whereby the field irrigation efficiency (indicating the fraction of irrigation water percolating to the underground) is to be taken into account.

The majority of the computer models available for water and solute transport in the soil (e.g. Swatre, DrainMod) are based on Richard's differential equation for the movement of water in unsaturated soil in combination with a differential salinity dispersion equation. The models require input of soil charac-teristics like the relation between unsaturated soil moisture content, water tension, hydraulic conductivity and dispersivity.

These relations vary to a great extent from place to place and are not easy to measure. The models use short time steps and need at least a daily data base of hydrological phenomena. Altogether this makes model application to a fairly large project the job of a team of specialists with ample facilities.

Soil Salinity Model: SaltMod

Saltmod is computer program for the prediction of the salinity of soil moisture, groundwater and drainage water, the depth of the watertable, and the drain discharge in irrigated agricultural lands, using different (geo) hydrologic conditions, varying water management options, including the use of ground water for irrigation, and several cropping rotation schedules. The water management options include irrigation, drainage, and the use of subsurface drainage water from pipe drains, ditches or wells for irrigation.

CHAPTER–13

Weathering

INTRODUCTION

Weathering is the decomposition of earth rocks, soils and their minerals through direct contact with the planet's atmosphere. Weathering occurs in situ, or "with no movement", and thus should not to be confused with erosion, which involves the movement of rocks and minerals by agents such as water, ice, wind, and gravity.

Two important classifications of weathering processes exist — physical and chemical weathering. Mechanical or physical weathering involves the breakdown of rocks and soils through direct contact with atmospheric conditions, such as heat, water, ice, and pressure. The second classification, chemical weathering, involves the direct effect of atmospheric chemicals or biologically produced chemicals (also known as biological weathering) in the breakdown of rocks, soils, and minerals.

The materials left over after the rock breaks down combined with organic material creates soil. The mineral content of the soil is determined by the parent material, thus a soil derived from a single rock type can often be deficient in one or more minerals for good fertility, while a soil weathered from a mix of rock types (as in glacial, eolian or alluvial sediments) often makes more fertile soil.

PHYSICAL (MECHANICAL) WEATHERING

Mechanical weathering is the cause of the disintegration of rocks. The primary process in mechanical weathering is abrasion (the process by which clasts and other particles are reduced in size). However, chemical and physical weathering often go hand in hand. For example, cracks exploited by mechanical weathering will increase the surface area exposed to chemical action. Furthermore, the chemical action at minerals in cracks can aid the disintegration process.

Thermal Expansion

Thermal expansion, also known as onion-skin weathering, exfoliation, insolation weathering or thermal shock, often occurs in areas, like deserts, where there is a large diurnal temperature range. The temperatures soar high in the day, while dipping greatly at night. As the rock heats up and expands by day, and cools and contracts by night, stress is often exerted on the outer layers. The stress causes the peeling off of the outer layers of rocks in thin sheets. Though this is caused mainly by temperature changes, thermal expansion is enhanced by the presence of moisture.

Frost Disintegration

This process can also be called frost shattering or frost-wedging. This type of weathering is common in mountain areas where the temperature is around freezing point. Frost induced weathering, although often attributed to the expansion of freezing water captured in cracks, is generally independent of the water-to-ice expansion. It has long been known that moist soils expand or frost heave upon freezing as a result of water migrating along from unfrozen areas via thin films to collect at growing ice lenses. This same phenomena occurs within pore spaces of rocks. They grow larger as they attract liquid water from the surrounding pores. The ice crystal growth weakens the rocks which, in time, break up. The phenomenon is caused by the almost unique property of water in having its greatest density at 4 C, so ice is of greater volume than water at the same temperature. When water freezes, then it expands and puts its surroundings under intense stress.

Freeze induced weathering action occurs mainly in environments where there is a lot of moisture, and temperatures frequently fluctuate above and below freezing point—that is, mainly alpine and periglacial areas. An example of rocks susceptible to frost action is chalk, which has many pore spaces for the growth of ice crystals. This process can be seen in Dartmoor where it results in the formation of tors. When water that has entered the joints freezes, the ice formed strains the walls of the joints and causes the joints to deepen and widen. This is because the volume of water expands by 9% when it freezes. When the ice thaws, water can flow further into the rock. When the temperature drops below freezing point and the water freezes again, the ice enlarges the joints further. Repeated freeze-thaw action weakens the rocks which, over time, break up along the joints into angular pieces. The angular rock fragments gather at the foot of the slope to form a talus slope (or scree slope). The splitting of rocks along the joints into blocks is called block disintegration. The blocks of rocks that are detached are of various shapes depending on rock structure.

Pressure Release

Pressure Release of granite.In pressure release, also known as unloading, overlying materials (not necessarily rocks) are removed (by erosion, or other processes), which causes underlying rocks to expand and fracture parallel to the surface. Often the overlying material is heavy, and the underlying rocks experience high pressure under them, for example, a moving glacier. Pressure release may also cause exfoliation to occur.

Intrusive igneous rocks (e.g. granite) are formed deep beneath the earth's surface. They are under tremendous pressure because of the overlying rock material. When erosion removes the overlying rock material, these intrusive rocks are exposed and the pressure on them is released. The outer parts of the rocks then tend to expand. The expansion sets up stresses which cause fractures parallel to the rock surface to form. Over time, sheets of rock break away from the exposed rocks along the fractures. Pressure release is also known as "exfoliation" or "sheeting"; these processes result in batholiths and granite domes, an example of which is Dartmoor.

Hydraulic Action

This is when water (generally from powerful waves) rushes into cracks in the rockface rapidly. This traps a layer of air at the bottom of the crack, compressing it and weakening the rock. When the wave retreats, the trapped air is suddenly released with explosive force. The explosive release of highly pressurized air cracks away fragments at the rockface and widens the crack itself.

SALT-CRYSTAL GROWTH (HALOCLASTY)

Salt weathering of sandstone near Qobustan, Azerbaijan.Salt crystallization or otherwise known as Haloclasty causes disintegration of rocks when saline (see salinity) solutions seep into cracks and joints in the rocks and evaporate, leaving salt crystals behind. These salt crystals expand as they are heated up, exerting pressure on the confining rock.

Salt crystallization may also take place when solutions decompose rocks (for example, limestone and chalk) to form salt solutions of sodium sulfate or sodium carbonate, of which the moisture evaporates to form their respective salt crystals.

The salts which have proved most effective in disintegrating rocks are sodium sulfate, magnesium sulfate, and calcium chloride. Some of these salts can expand up to three times or even more.

It is normally associated with arid climates where strong heating causes strong evaporation and therefore salt crystallization. It is also common along coasts. An example of salt weathering can be seen in the honeycombed stones in sea wall. Honeycomb is a type of tafoni, a class of cavernous rock weathering structures, which likely develop in large part by chemical and physical salt weathering processes.

Biological Weathering

Lichens and mosses grow on essentially bare rock surfaces and create a more humid chemical microenvironment. The attachment of these organisms to the rock surface enhances physical as well as chemical breakdown of the surface microlayer of the rock. On a larger scale seedlings sprouting in a crevice and plant roots exert physical pressure as well as providing a pathway for water and chemical infiltration. Burrowing animals and insects disturb the soil layer adjacent to the bedrock surface thus further increasing water and acid infiltration and exposure to oxidation processes.

CHEMICAL WEATHERING

Chemical weathering involves the change in the composition of rocks, often leading to a 'break down' in its form. This is done through a combination of water and various chemicals to create an acid which directly breaks down the material. This type of weathering happens over a period of time. Chemical weathering may alter a rock's chemical make up by changing the minerals in the rock or it adds some new minerals.

Dissolution

Rainfall is acidic because atmospheric carbon dioxide dissolves in the rainwater producing weak carbonic acid. In unpolluted environments, the rainfall pH is around 5.6. Acid rain occurs when gases such as sulphur dioxide and nitrogen oxides are present in the atmosphere. These oxides react in the rain water to produce stronger acids and can lower the pH to 4.5 or even 3.0. Sulfur dioxide, SO_2, comes from volcanic eruptions or from fossil fuels, can become sulfuric acid within rainwater, which can cause solution weathering to the rocks on which it falls.

One of the most well-known solution weathering processes is carbonation, the process in which atmospheric carbon dioxide leads to solution weathering. Carbonation occurs on rocks which contain calcium carbonate, such as limestone and chalk. This takes place when rain combines with carbon dioxide or an organic acid to form a weak carbonic acid which reacts with calcium carbonate (the limestone) and forms calcium bicarbonate. This process speeds up with a decrease in temperature and therefore is a large feature of glacial weathering.

The reactions as follows:

$$CO_2 + H_2O \rightarrow H_2CO_3$$

carbon dioxide + water → carbonic acid

$$H_2CO_3 + CaCO_3 \rightarrow Ca(HCO_3)_2$$

carbonic acid + calcium carbonate → calcium bicarbonate

Carbonation on the surface of well-jointed limestone produces a dissected limestone pavement which is most effective along the joints, widening and deepening them.

Hydration

Mineral hydration is a form of chemical weathering that involves the rigid attachment of H^+ and OH^- ions to the atoms and molecules of a mineral.

When rock minerals take up water, the increased volume creates physical stresses within the rock. For example iron oxides are converted to iron hydroxides and the hydration of anhydrite forms gypsum.

A freshly broken rock shows differential chemical weathering (probably mostly oxidation) progressing inward. This piece of sandstone was found in glacial drift near Angelica, New York.

Hydrolysis

Hydrolysis is a chemical weathering process affecting Silicate minerals. In such reactions, pure water ionizes slightly and reacts with silicate minerals. An example reaction:

$$Mg_2SiO_4 + 4H^+ + 4OH^- \rightarrow 2Mg_2^+ + 4OH^- + H_4SiO_4$$

olivine (forsterite) + four ionized water molecules ? ions in solution + silicic acid in solution

This reaction results in complete dissolution of the original mineral, assuming enough water is available to drive the reaction. However, the above reaction is to a degree deceptive because pure water rarely acts as a H+ donor. Carbon dioxide, though, dissolves readily in water forming a weak acid and H+ donor.

$$Mg_2SiO_4 + 4CO_2 + 4H_2O \rightarrow 2Mg_2^+ + 4HCO_3^- + H_4SiO_4$$

olivine (forsterite) + carbon dioxide + water → Magnesium and bicarbonate ions in solution + silicic acid in solution

This hydrolysis reaction is much more common. Carbonic acid is consumed by silicate weathering, resulting in more alkaline solutions because of the bicarbonate. This is an important reaction in controlling the amount of CO_2 in the atmosphere and can affect climate.

Aluvinosilicates when subjected to the hydrolysis reaction produce a secondary mineral rather than simply releasing cations.

Orthoclase (aluminosilicate feldspar) + carbonic acid + water → Kaolinite (a clay mineral) + silicic acid in solution + potassium and bicarbonate ions in solution.

Oxidation

Within the weathering environment chemical oxidation of a variety of metals occurs. The most commonly observed is the oxidation of Fe_2^+ (iron) and combination with oxygen and water to form Fe_3^+ hydroxides and oxides such as goethite, limonite, and hematite. This gives the affected rocks a reddish-brown colouration on the surface which crumbles easily and weakens the rock. This process is better known as 'rusting'. Many other metallic ores and minerals oxidize and hydrate to produce coloured deposits, such as chalcopyrites or $CuFeS_2$ oxidizing to copper hydroxide and iron oxides.

Biological

A number of plants and animals may create chemical weathering through release of acidic compounds, i.e moss on roofs is classed as weathering.

The most common form of biological weathering is the release of chelating compounds, i.e acids, by plants so as to break down aluminium and iron containing compounds in the soils beneath them. Decaying remains of dead plants in soil may form organic acids which, when dissolved in water, cause chemical weathering. Extreme release of chelating compounds can easily affect surrounding rocks and soils, and may lead to podsolisation of soils.

Carbonation

Carbonation occurs in rocks with a high content of calcium carbonate such as limestone and chalk. Carbon dioxide from the atmosphere combines with water to produce a weak acid called carbonic acid. This acid reacts with the calcium carbonate to form calcium bicarbonate. Calcium bicarbonate is soluble so therefore the rock is dissolved and carried away. This type of weathering can produce landforms such as caves, limestone pavements and sinkholes.

Building Weathering

Buildings made of any stone, brick or concrete are susceptible to the same weathering agents as any exposed rock surface. Also statues, monuments and ornamental stonework can be badly damaged by natural weathering processes. This is accelerated in areas severely affected by acid rain.

EROSION

Erosion is the carrying away or displacement of solids (sediment, soil, rock and other particles) usually by the agents of currents such as, wind, water, or ice by downward or down-slope movement in response to gravity or by living organisms (in the case of bioerosion).

Erosion is distinguished from weathering, which is the process of chemical or physical breakdown of the minerals in the rocks, although the two processes may be concurrent.

Erosion is a noticeable intrinsic natural process but in many places it is increased by human land use. Poor land use practices include deforestation, overgrazing, unmanaged construction activity and road-building. Land that is used for the production of agricultural crops generally experiences a significant greater rate of erosion than that of land under natural vegetation. This is particularly true if tillage is used, which reduces vegetation cover on the surface of the soil and disturbs both soil structure and plant roots that would otherwise hold the soil in place. However, improved land use practices can limit erosion, using techniques such as terrace-building, conservation tillage practices, and tree planting.

A certain amount of erosion is natural and, in fact, healthy for the ecosystem. For example, gravels continuously move downstream in watercourses. Excessive erosion, however, does cause problems, such as receiving water sedimentation, ecosystem damage and outright loss of soil.

Causes

Soil erosion exposing rootsThe rate of erosion depends on many factors. Climatic factors include the amount and intensity of precipitation, the average temperature, as well as the typical temperature range, and seasonality, the wind speed, storm frequency. The geologic factors include the sediment or rock type, its porosity and permeability, the slope (gradient) of the land, and if the rocks are tilted, faulted, folded, or weathered. The biological factors include ground cover from vegetation or lack thereof, the type of organisms inhabiting the area, and the land use.

In general, given vegetation and ecosystems, you expect areas with high-intensity precipitation, more frequent rainfall, more wind, or more storms to have more erosion. Sediment with high sand or silt contents and areas with steep slopes erode more easily, as do areas with highly fractured or weathered rock. Porosity and permeability of the sediment or rock affect the speed with which the water can percolate into the ground. If the water moves underground, less runoff is generated, reducing the amount of surface erosion. Sediment containing more clay tend to erode less than those with sand or silt. Here, however, the impact of atmospheric sodium on erodibility of clay should be considered.

The factor that is most subject to change is the amount and type of ground cover. In an undisturbed forest, the mineral soil is protected by a litter layer and an organic layer. These two layers protect the soil by absorbing the impact of rain drops. These layers and the underlaying soil in a forest is porous and highly permeable to rainfall. Typically only the most severe rainfall and large hailstorm events will lead to overland flow in a forest. If the trees are removed by fire or logging, infiltration rates remain high and erosion low to the degree the forest floor remains intact. Severe fires can lead to significantly increased erosion if followed by heavy rainfall. In the case of construction or road building when the litter layer is removed or compacted the susceptibility of the soil to erosion is greatly increased.

Roads are especially likely to cause increased rates of erosion because, in addition to removing ground cover, they can significantly change drainage patterns especially if an embankment has been made to support the road. A road that has a lot of rock and one that is "hydrologically invisible" (that gets the water off the road as quickly as possible, mimicking natural drainage patterns) has the best chance of not causing increased erosion.

Many human activities remove vegetation from an area, making the soil easily eroded. Logging can cause increased erosion rates due to soil compaction, exposure of mineral soil, for example roads and landings. However it is the removal of or compromise to the forest floor not the removal of the canopy that can lead to erosion. This is because rain drops striking tree leaves coalesce with other rain drops creating larger drops. When these larger drops fall (called throughfall) they again may reach terminal velocity and strike the ground with more energy then had they fallen in the open. Terminal velocity of rain drops is reached in about 8 meters. Because forest canopies are usually higher than this, leaf drop can regain terminal velocity. However, the intact forest floor, with its layers of leaf litter and organic matter, absorbs the impact of the rainfall.

Heavy grazing can reduce vegetation enough to increase erosion. Changes in the kind of vegetation in an area can also affect erosion rates. Different kinds of vegetation lead to different infiltration rates of rain into the soil. Forested areas have higher infiltration rates, so precipitation will result in less surface runoff, which erodes. Instead much of the water will go in subsurface flows, which are generally less erosive. Leaf litter and low shrubs are an important part of the high infiltration rates of forested systems, the removal of which can increase erosion rates. Leaf litter also shelters the soil from the impact of falling raindrops, which is a significant agent of erosion. Vegetation can also change the speed of surface runoff flows, so grasses and shrubs can also be instrumental in this aspect.

One of the main causes of erosive soil loss in the year 2006 is the result of slash and burn treatment of tropical forest. When the total ground surface is stripped of vegetation and then seared of all living organisms, the upper soils are vulnerable to both wind and water erosion. In a number of regions of the earth, entire sectors of a country have been rendered unproductive. For example, on the Madagascar high central plateau, comprising approximately ten percent of that country's land area, virtually the entire landscape is sterile of vegetation, with gully erosive furrows typically in excess of 50 meters deep and one kilometer wide. Shifting cultivation is a farming system which sometimes incorporates the slash and burn method in some regions of the world. This degrades the soil and causes the soil to become less and less fertile.

Effects

Approximately 40% of the world's agricultural land is seriously degraded. According to the UN, an area of fertile soil the size of Ukraine is lost every year because of drought, deforestation and climate change.In Africa, if current trends of soil degradation continue, the continent might be able to feed just 25% of its population by 2025, according to UNU's Ghana-based Institute for Natural Resources in Africa.

Bank erosion started by four wheeler all-terrain vehicles, Yauhanna, South CarolinaWhen land is overused by animal activities (including humans), there can be mechanical erosion and also removal of vegetation leading to erosion. In the case of the animal kingdom, this effect would become material primarily with very large animal herds stampeding such as the Blue Wildebeest on the Serengeti plain. Even in this case there are broader material benefits to the ecosystem, such as continuing the survival of grasslands, that are indigenous to this region. This effect may be viewed as anomalous or a problem only when there is a significant imbalance or overpopulation of one species.

In the case of human use, the effects are also generally linked to overpopulation. When large number of hikers use trails or extensive off road vehicle use occurs, erosive effects often follow, arising from vegetation removal and furrowing of foot traffic and off road vehicle tires. These effects can also accumulate from a variety of outdoor human activities, again simply arising from too many people using a finite land resource.

One of the most serious and long-running water erosion problems worldwide is in the People's Republic of China, on the middle reaches of the Yellow River and the upper reaches of the Yangtze River. From the Yellow River, over 1.6 billion tons of sediment flows into the ocean each year. The sediment originates primarily from water erosion in the Loess Plateau region of the northwest.

EROSION PROCESSES

Gravity Erosion

Mass wasting is the down-slope movement of rock and sediments, mainly due to the force of gravity. Mass movement is an important part of the erosional process, as it moves material from higher elevations to lower elevations where other eroding agents such as streams and glaciers can then pick up the material and move it to even lower elevations. Mass-movement processes are always occurring continuously on all slopes; some mass-movement processes act very slowly; others occur very suddenly, often with disastrous results. Any perceptible down-slope movement of rock or sediment is often referred to in general terms as a landslide. However, landslides can be classified in a much more detailed way that reflects the mechanisms responsible for the movement and the velocity at which the movement occurs. One of the visible topographical manifestations of a very slow form of such activity is a scree slope.

Slumping happens on steep hillsides, occurring along distinct fracture zones, often within materials like clay that, once released, may move quite rapidly downhill. They will often show a spoon-shaped isostatic depression, in which the material has begun to slide downhill. In some cases, the slump is caused by water beneath the slope weakening it. In many cases it is simply the result of poor engineering along highways where it is a regular occurrence.

Surface creep is the slow movement of soil and rock debris by gravity which is usually not perceptible except through extended observation. However, the term can also describe the rolling of dislodged soil particles 0.5 to 1.0 mm in diameter by wind along the soil surface.

Water Erosion

Nearly perfect sphere in granite, Trégastel, Brittany. Splash erosion is the detachment and airborne movement of small soil particles caused by the impact of raindrops on soil.

Sheet erosion is the detachment of soil particles by raindrop impact and their removal downslope by water flowing overland as a sheet instead of in definite channels or rills. The impact of the raindrop breaks apart the soil aggregate. Particles of clay, silt and sand fill the soil pores and reduce infiltration. After the surface pores are filled with sand, silt or clay, overland surface flow of water begins due to the lowering of infiltration rates. Once the rate of falling rain is faster than infiltration, runoff takes place. There are two stages of sheet erosion. The first is rain splash, in which soil particles are knocked into the air by raindrop impact. In the second stage, the loose particles are moved downslope by broad sheets of rapidly flowing water filled with sediment known as sheetfloods. This stage of sheet erosion is generally produced by cloudbursts, sheetfloods commonly travel short distances and last only for a short time.

Rill erosion refers to the development of small, ephemeral concentrated flow paths, which function as both sediment source and sediment delivery systems for erosion on hillslopes. Generally, where water erosion rates on disturbed upland areas are greatest, rills are active. Flow depths in rills are typically on the order of a few centimeters or less and slopes may be quite steep. These conditions constitute a very different hydraulic environment than typically found in channels of streams and rivers. Eroding rills evolve morphologically in time and space. The rill bed surface changes as soil erodes, which in turn alters the hydraulics of the flow. The hydraulics is the driving mechanism for the erosion process, and therefore dynamically changing hydraulic patterns cause continually changing erosional patterns in the rill. Thus, the process of rill evolution involves a feedback loop between flow detachment, hydraulics, and bed form. Flow velocity, depth, width, hydraulic roughness, local bed slope, friction slope, and detachment rate are time and space variable functions of the rill evolutionary process. Superimposed on these interactive processes, the sediment load, or amount of sediment in the flow, has a large influence on soil detachment rates in rills. As sediment load increases, the ability of the flowing water to detach more sediment decreases.

Where precipitation rates exceed soil infiltration rates, runoff occurs. Surface runoff turbulence can often cause more erosion than the initial raindrop impact.

Gully erosion results where water flows along a linear depression eroding a trench or gully. This is particularly noticeable in the formation of hollow ways, where, prior to being tarmacked, an old rural road has over many years become significantly lower than the surrounding fields.

Valley or stream erosion occurs with continued water flow along a linear feature. The erosion is both downward, deepening the valley, and headward, extending the valley into the hillside. In the earliest stage of stream erosion, the erosive activity is dominantly vertical, the valleys have a typical V cross-section and the stream gradient is relatively steep. When some base level is reached, the erosive activity switches to lateral erosion, which widens the valley floor and creates a narrow floodplain. The stream gradient becomes nearly flat, and lateral deposition of sediments becomes important as the stream meanders across the valley floor. In all stages of stream erosion, by far the most erosion occurs during times of flood, when more and faster-moving water is available to carry a larger sediment load. In such processes, it is not the water alone that erodes: suspended abrasive particles, pebbles and boulders can also act erosively as they traverse a surface.

At extremely high flows, kolks, or vortices are formed by large volumes of rapidly rushing water. Kolks cause extreme local erosion, plucking bedrock and creating pothole-type geographical features called Rock-cut basins. Examples can be seen in the flood regions result from glacial Lake Missoula, which created the channeled scablands in the Columbia Basin region of eastern Washington.

Shoreline Erosion

Wave cut platform caused by erosion of cliffs by the sea, at Southerndown in South WalesShoreline erosion, which occurs on both exposed and sheltered coasts, primarily occurs through the action of currents and waves but sea level (tidal) change can also play a role.

Hydraulic action takes place when air in a joint is suddenly compressed by a wave closing the entrance of the joint. This then cracks it. Wave pounding is when the sheer energy of the wave hitting the cliff or rock breaks pieces off. Abrasion or corrasion is caused by waves launching seaload at the cliff. It is the most effective and rapid form of shoreline erosion (not to be confused with corrosion). Corrosion is the dissolving of rock by carbonic acid in sea water. Limestone cliffs are particularly vulnerable to this kind of erosion. Attrition is where particles/seaload carried by the waves are worn down as they hit each other and the cliffs. This then makes the material easier to wash away. The material ends up as shingle and sand. Another significant source of erosion, particularly on carbonate coastlines, is the boring, scraping and grinding of organisms, a process termed bioerosion.

Sediment is transported along the coast in the direction of the prevailing current (longshore drift). When the upcurrent amount of sediment is less than the amount being carried away, erosion occurs. When the upcurrent amount of sediment is greater, sand or gravel banks will tend to form. These banks may slowly migrate along the coast in the direction of the longshore drift, alternately protecting and exposing parts of the coastline. Where there is a bend in the coastline, quite often a build up of eroded material occurs forming a long narrow bank (a spit). armored beaches and submerged offshore sandbanks may also protect parts of a coastline from erosion. Over the years, as the shoals gradually shift, the erosion may be redirected to attack different parts of the shore.

Ice Erosion

Ice erosion is caused by movement of ice, typically as glaciers. Glaciers erode predominantly by three different processes: abrasion/scouring, plucking, and ice thrusting. In an abrasion process, debris in the basal ice scrapes along the bed, polishing and gouging the underlying rocks, similar to sandpaper on wood. Glaciers can also cause pieces of bedrock to crack off in the process of plucking. In ice thrusting, the glacier freezes to its bed, then as it surges forward, it moves large sheets of frozen sediment at the base along with the glacier. This method produced some of the many thousands of lake basins that dot the edge of the Canadian Shield. These processes, combined with erosion and transport by the water network beneath the glacier, leave moraines, drumlins, eskers, ground moraine (till), kames, kame deltas, moulins, and glacial erratics in their wake, typically at the terminus or during glacier retreat.

Cold weather causes water trapped in tiny rock cracks to freeze and expand, breaking the rock into several pieces. This can lead to gravity erosion on steep slopes. The scree which forms at the bottom of a steep mountainside is mostly formed from pieces of rock (soil) broken away by this means. It is a common engineering problem wherever rock cliffs are alongside roads, because morning thaws can drop hazardous rock pieces onto the road.

In some places, water seeps into rocks during the daytime, then freezes at night. Ice expands, thus, creating a wedge in the rock. Over time, the repetition in the forming and melting of the ice causes fissures, which eventually breaks the rock down.

Wind Erosion

A rock formation in the Altiplano, Bolivia sculpted by wind erosion.

Wind erosion is the result of material movement by the wind. There are two main effects. First, wind causes small particles to be lifted and therefore moved to another region. This is called deflation. Second, these suspended particles may impact on solid objects causing erosion by abrasion (ecological succession).

Wind erosion generally occurs in areas with little or no vegetation, often in areas where there is insufficient rainfall to support vegetation. An example is the formation of sand dunes, on a beach or in a desert. Windbreaks (such as big trees and bushes) are often planted by farmers to reduce wind erosion.

Soil Erosion and Climate Change

The consensus of atmospheric scientists is that climate change is occurring, both in terms of global air temperature and precipitation patterns. Warmer atmospheric temperatures associated with greenhouse warming are expected to lead to a more vigorous hydrological cycle, including more extreme rainfall events. In 1998 Karl and Knight reported that from 1910 to 1996 total precipitation over the contiguous U.S. increased, and that 53% of the increase came from the upper 10% of precipitation events (the most intense precipitation). The percent of precipitation coming from days of precipitation in excess of 50 mm has also increased significantly.

Studies on soil erosion suggest that increased rainfall amounts and intensities will lead to greater rates of erosion. Thus, if rainfall amounts and intensities increase in many parts of the world as expected, erosion will also increase, unless amelioration measures are taken. Soil erosion rates are expected to change in response to changes in climate for a variety of reasons. The most direct is the change in the erosive power of rainfall. Other reasons include: (a) changes plant canopy caused by shifts in plant biomass production associated with moisture regime; (b) changes in litter cover on the ground caused by changes in both plant residue decomposition rates driven by temperature and moisture dependent soil microbial activity as well as plant biomass production rates; (c) changes in soil moisture due to shifting precipitation regimes and evapo-transpiration rates, which changes infiltration and runoff ratios; (d) soil erodibility changes due to decrease in soil organic matter concentrations in soils that lead to a soil structure that is more susceptible to erosion and increased runoff due to increased soil surface sealing and crusting; (e) a shift of winter precipitation from non-erosive snow to erosive rainfall due to increasing winter temperatures; (f) melting of permafrost, which induces an erodible soil state from a previously non-erodible one; and (g) shifts in land use made necessary to accommodate new climatic regimes.

Studies by Pruski and Nearing indicated that, other factors such as land use not considered, we can expect approximately a 1.7% change in soil erosion for each 1% change in total precipitation under climate change

Tectonic Effects of Erosion

The removal by erosion of large amounts of rock from a particular region, and its deposition elsewhere, can result in a lightening of the load on the lower crust and mantle. This can cause tectonic or isostatic uplift in the region. Research undertaken since the early 1990s suggests that the spatial distribution of erosion at the surface of an orogen can exert a key influence on its growth and its final internal structure (see erosion and tectonics).

Materials Science

In materials science, erosion is the recession of surfaces by repeated localized mechanical trauma as, for example, by suspended abrasive particles within a moving fluid. Erosion can also occur from non-abrasive fluid mixtures. Cavitation is one example.

In hard particle erosion, the hardness of the impacted material is a large factor in the mechanics of the erosion. A soft material will typically erode fastest from glancing impacts. Harder material will typically erode fastest from perpendicular impacts. Hardness is a correlative factor for erosion resistance, but a higher hardness does not guarantee better resistance. Factors that affect the erosion rate also include impacting particle speed, size, density, hardness, and rotation. Coatings can be applied to retard erosion, but normally can only slow the removal of material. Erosion rate for solid particle impact is typically measured as mass of material removed divided by the mass of impacting material

Figurative Use

The concept of erosion is commonly employed by analogy to various forms of perceived or real homogenization (i.e. erosion of boundaries), "leveling out", collusion or even the decline of anything from morals to indigenous cultures. It is a common trope of the English language to describe as erosion the gradual, organic mutation of something thought of as distinct, more complex, harder to pronounce or more refined into something indistinct, less complex, easier to pronounce or (disparagingly) less refined.

Origin of Term

The first known occurrence of the term "erosion" was in the 1541 translation by Robert Copland of Guy de Chauliac's medical text The Questyonary of Cyrurygens. Copland used erosion to describe how ulcers developed in the mouth. By 1774 'erosion' was used outside medical subjects. Oliver Goldsmith employed the term in the more contemporary geological context, in his book Natural History, with the quote.

Bounds are thus put to the erosion of the earth by water.

CHAPTER–14
Soil Contamination

INTRODUCTION

Soil contamination is caused by the presence of man-made chemicals or other alteration in the natural soil environment. This type of contamination typically arises from the rupture of underground storage tanks, application of pesticides, percolation of contaminated surface water to subsurface strata, oil and fuel dumping, leaching of wastes from landfills or direct discharge of industrial wastes to the soil. The most common chemicals involved are petroleum hydrocarbons, solvents, pesticides, lead and other heavy metals. This occurrence of this phenomenon is correlated with the degree of industrialization and intensity of chemical usage.

The concern over soil contamination stems primarily from health risks, both of direct contact and from secondary contamination of water supplies Mapping of contaminated soil sites and the resulting cleanup are time consuming and expensive tasks, requiring extensive amounts of geology, hydrology, chemistry and computer modeling skills.

It is in North America and Western Europe that the extent of contaminated land is most well known, with many of countries in these areas having a legal framework to identify and deal with this environmental problem; this however may well be just the tip of the iceberg with developing countries very likely to be the next generation of new soil contamination cases.

The immense and sustained growth of the People's Republic of China since the 1970s has exacted a price from the land in increased soil pollution. The State Environmental Protection Administration believes it to be a threat to the environment, to food safety and to sustainable agriculture. According to a scientific sampling, 150 million mi (100,000 square kilometres) of China's cultivated land have been polluted, with contaminated water being used to irrigate a further 32.5 million mi (21,670 square kilometres) and another 2 million mi (1,300 square kilometres) covered or destroyed by solid waste. In total, the area accounts for one-tenth of China's cultivatable land, and is mostly in economically developed areas. An estimated 12 million tonnes of grain are contaminated by heavy metals every year, causing direct losses of 20 billion yuan (US$2.57 billion).

The United States, while having some of the most widespread soil contamination, has actually been a leader in defining and implementing standards for cleanup Other industrialized countries have a large number of contaminated sites, but lag the U.S. in executing remediation. Developing countries may be leading in the next generation of new soil contamination cases.

Each year in the U.S., thousands of sites complete soil contamination cleanup, some by using microbes that "eat up" toxic chemicals in soil[4], many others by simple excavation and others by more expensive high-tech soil vapor extraction or air stripping. At the same time, efforts proceed worldwide in creating and identifying new sites of soil contamination, particularly in industrial countries other than the U.S., and in developing countries which lack the money and the technology to adequately protect soil resources.

Health Effects

The major concern is that there are many sensitive land uses where people are in direct contact with soils such as residences, parks, schools and playgrounds. Other contact mechanisms include contamination of drinking water or inhalation of soil contaminants which have vaporized.

There is a very large set of health consequences from exposure to soil contamination depending on pollutant type, pathway of attack and vulnerability of the exposed population . Chromium and obsolete pesticide formulations are carcinogenic to populations[citation needed]. Lead is especially hazardous to young children, in which group there is a high risk of developmental damage to the brain, while to all populations kidney damage is a risk.

Chronic exposure to at sufficient concentrations is known to be associated with higher incidence of leukemia. Obsolete pesticides such as mercury and cyclodienes are known to induce higher incidences of kidney damage, some irreversible; cyclodienes are linked to liver toxicity. Organophosphates and carbamates can induce a chain of responses leading to neuromuscular blockage.

Many chlorinated solvents induce liver changes, kidney changes and depression of the central nervous system. There is an entire spectrum of further health effects such as headache, nausea, physical fatigue, eye irritation and skin rash for the above cited and other chemicals.

ECOSYSTEM EFFECTS

Not unexpectedly, soil contaminants can have significant deleterious consequences for ecosystems. There are radical soil chemistry changes which can arise from the presence of many hazardous chemicals even at low concentration of the contaminant species. These changes can manifest in the alteration of metabolism of endemic microorganisms and arthropods resident in a given soil environment. The result can be virtual eradication of some of the primary food chain, which in turn have major consequences for predator or consumer species. Even if the chemical effect on lower life forms is small, the lower pyramid levels of the food chain may ingest alien chemicals, which normally become more concentrated for each consuming rung of the food chain. Many of these effects are now well known, such as the concentration of persistent DDT materials for avian consumers, leading to weakening of egg shells, increased chick mortality and potentially species extinction.

Effects occur to agricultural lands which have certain types of soil contamination. Contaminants typically alter plant metabolism, most commonly to reduce crop yields. This has a secondary effect upon soil conservation, since the languishing crops cannot shield the earth's soil mantle from erosion phenomena. Some of these chemical contaminants have long half-lives and in other cases derivative chemicals are formed from decay of primary soil contaminants.

Regulatory Framework

Until about 1970 there was little widespread awareness of the worldwide scope of soil contamination or its health risks. In fact, areas of concern were often viewed as unusual or isolated incidents. Since then, the U.S. has established guidelines for handling hazardous waste and the cleanup of soil pollution. In 1980 the U.S.Superfund/CERCLA established strict rules on legal liability for soil contamination. Not only did CERCLA stimulate identification and cleanup of thousands of sites, but it raised awareness of property buyers and sellers to make soil pollution a focal issue of land use and management practices.

While estimates of remaining soil cleanup in the U.S. may exceed 200,000 sites, in other industrialized countries there is a lag of identification and cleanup functions. Even though their use of chemicals is lower than industrialized countries, often their controls and regulatory framework is quite weak. For example, some persistent pesticides that have been banned in the U.S. are in widespread uncontrolled use in developing countries. It is worth noting that the cost of cleaning up a soil contaminated site can range from as little as about $10,000 for a small spill, which can be simply excavated, to millions of dollars for a widespread event, especially for a chemical that is very mobile such as perchloroethylene.

China

China, an economy that regularly records double digit annual economic growth, has little or no legislation to protect the environment. Currently, given the amount of land in question (up to one-tenth of China's cultivatable land may be polluted), the degree of the pollution in specific locations is unclear, making both prevention and remedy difficult. There are no laws or environmental standards regarding soil. Funding is limited, too, so there is little advanced scientific study of China's soil taking place. The severity of the pollution is not known by the public or business population, and the situation is most likely worsening as a result.

United Kingdom

Generic guidance commonly used in the UK are the Soil Guideline Values published by DEFRA and the Environment Agency. These are screening values that demonstrate the minimal acceptable level of a substance. Above this there can be no assurances in terms of significant risk of harm to human health. These have been derived using the Contaminated Land Exposure Asseeement Model (CLEA UK). Certain input parameters such as Health Criteria Values, age and land use are fed into CLEA UK to obtain a probablistic output[citation needed].

Guidance by the Inter Departmental Committee for the Redevelopment of Contaminated Land (ICRCL) has been formally withdrawn by the Department for Environment, Food and Rural Affairs (DEFRA), for use as a prescriptive document to determine the potential need for remediation or further assessment. Therefore, no further reference is made to these former guideline values.

Other generic guidance that exists (to put the concentration of a particular contaminant in context), includes the United States EPA Region 9 Preliminary Remediation Goals (US PRGs), the US EPA Region 3 Risk Based Concentrations (US EPA RBCs) and National Environment Protection Council of Australia Guideline on Investigation Levels in Soil and Groundwater.

However international guidance should only be used in the UK with clear justification. This is because foreign standards are usually particular to that country due to drivers such as political policy, geology, flood regime and epidemiology. It is generally accepted by UK regulators that only robust scientific methods that relate to the UK should be used.

The CLEA model published by DEFRA and the Environment Agency (EA) in March 2002 sets a framework for the appropriate assessment of risks to human health from contaminated land, as required by Part IIA of the Environmental Protection Act 1990. As part of this framework, generic Soil Guideline Values (SGVs) have currently been derived for ten contaminants to be used as "intervention values". These values should not be considered as remedial targets but values above which further detailed assessment should be considered.

Three sets of CLEA SGVs have been produced for three different land-uses, namely:

- residential (with and without plant uptake);
- allotments; and
- commercial/industrial.

It is intended that the SGVs replace the former ICRCL values. It should be noted that the CLEA SGVs relate to assessing chronic (long term) risks to human health and do not apply to the protection of ground workers during construction, or other potential receptors such as groundwater, buildings, plants or other ecosystems. The CLEA SGVs are not directly applicable to a site completely covered in hardstanding, as there is no direct exposure route to contaminated soils.

To date, the first ten of fifty-five contaminant SGVs have been published, for the following: arsenic, cadmium, chromium, lead, inorganic mercury, nickel, selenium ethyl benzene, phenol and toluene. Draft SGVs for benzene, naphthalene and xylene have been produced but their publication is on hold. Toxicological data (Tox) has been published for each of these contaminants as well as for benzo[a]pyrene, benzene, dioxins, furans and dioxin-like PCBs, naphthalene, vinyl chloride, 1, 1, 2, 2 tetrachloroethane and 1, 1, 1, 2 tetrachloroethane, 1, 1, 1 trichloroethane, tetrachloroethene, carbon tetrachloride, 1, 2-dichloroethane, trichloroethene and xylene. The SGVs for ethyl benzene, phenol and toluene are dependent on the soil organic matter (SOM) content (which can be calculated from the total organic carbon (TOC) content). As an initial screen the SGVs for 1% SOM are considered to be appropriate.

Cleanup Options

Microbes can be used in soil cleanupCleanup or remediation is analyzed by environmental scientists who utilize field measurement of soil chemicals and also apply computer models for analyzing transport and fate of soil chemicals. Thousands of soil contamination cases are currently in active cleanup across the U.S. as of 2006. There are several principal strategies for remediation:

- Excavate soil and remove it to a disposal site away from ready pathways for human or sensitive ecosystem contact. This technique also applies to dredging of bay muds containing toxins.
- Aeration of soils at the contaminated site (with attendant risk of creating air pollution)

Thermal remediation by introduction of heat to raise subsurface temperatures sufficiently high to volatize chemical contaminants out of the soil for vapour extraction. Technologies include ISTD, electrical resistance heating (ERH), and ET-DSPtm.

Bioremediation, involving microbial digestion of certain organic chemicals. Techniques used in bioremediation include landfarming, biostimulation and bioaugmentation soil biota with commercially available microflora.

Extraction of groundwater or soil vapor with an active electromechanical system, with subsequent stripping of the contaminants from the extract.

Containment of the soil contaminants (such as by capping or paving over in place).

LAND POLLUTION

Land pollution is the degradation of earth's land surfaces often caused by human activities and their misuse of land resources. Haphazard disposal of urban and industrial wastes, exploitation of minerals, and improper use of soil by inadequate agricultural practices are a few factors. Urbanization and industrialisation are major causes of land pollution.

The Industrial Revolution set a series of events into motion which destroyed natural habitats and polluted the environment, causing diseases in both humans and animals.

Increased Mechanisation

In some areas, metal ores are extracted from the ground, melted, cast and cooled using river water, which raises the temperature of water in rivers. This reduces the oxygen carrying capacity of the water and affects the aquatic life forms. The excavation of minerals leads to a large scale quarrying and defacing of land. To a large extent, this has been stopped or is more controlled, and attempts have been made to use the quarries profitably e.g. sand pits have been turned into boating lochs and some have been used as landfills. Central Scotland bears the scars of years of coal mining, with pit binges and slag heaps visible from the motorways.

The increase in the concentration of population in cities, along wit the internal combustion engine, led to the increased number of roas and all the infra structure that goes with them. Roads cause visual, noise, light, air and water pollution, in addition to land pollution. The visual and noise areas are obvious, however light ollution is becoming more widely recognised as a problem. From uter space, large cities can be picked out at night by the glowof their lighting, so city dwellers seldom experience total darkness.

The cntribution of vehicular traffic to air pollution is dealt with in another article, but, suffice to say that sulfur dioxide, nitrogen oxide and carbon monoxide are the main culprits. Water pollution is caused by the run off from roads of oil, salt and rubber residue, which enter the water courses and may make conditions unsuitable for certain organisms to live.

As thedemand for food has grown very high, there is an increas in field size and mechanization. The increase in field size makes it economically viable for the farmer but results in loss of habitat and shelter for wildlife, as hedgerows and copses disappear. When crops are harvested, the naked soil is left open to wind after the heavy machinery has compacted it. Another consequence of more intensive agriculture is the move to monoculture. This is unnatural, it depletes the soil of nutrients, allows diseases and pests to spread and, in short, brings into play the use of chemical substances foreign to the environment.

Pesticides

Pesticides are chemicals used to kill pests. These can cause soil contamination and water contamination as well. Pesticides are the chemical used for spaying to the crop. It kills the insects near by the crop which affects the crop. The biggest drawback of the pesticide is that after a certain period of time the fertility of land goes away.

Herbicides

Herbicides are used to kill weeds, especially on pavements and railways. They are similar to auxins and most are biodegradable by soil bacteria. However one group derived from trinitrophenol (2 : 4 D and 2 : 4 : 5 T) have the impurity dioxin, which is very toxic and causes fatality even in low concentrations. It also causes spontaneous abortions, haemorrhaging and cancer. Agent Orange (50% 2 : 4 : 5 T) was used as a defoliant in Vietnam. Eleven million gallons were used and children born since then to American soldiers who served in this conflict, have shown increased physical and mental disabilities compared to the rest of the population. It affects the head of the sperm and the chromosomes inside it.

Another herbicide, much loved by murder story writers, is Paraquat. It is highly toxic but it rapidly degrades in soil due to the action of bacteria and does not kill soil fauna.

Fungicides

Fungicides are the group used to stop the growth of smuts and rusts on cereals, and mildews and moulds like Mucor on plants. The problem is that they may contain copper and mercury. Copper is very toxic (at 1ppm) to water plants and fish, and can enter human skin if sprayed and accumulate in the central nervous system. Organomercury compounds have been used to get rid of sedges, which are insidious and difficult to remove. However it also can accumulate in birds' central nervous systems and kill them.

Insecticides

Insecticides are used to rid farms of pests which damage crops. The insects damage not only standing crops but also stored ones and in the tropics it is reckoned that one third of the total production is lost during food storage. As with fungicides, the first insecticides used in the nineteenth century were inorganic e.g. Paris Green and other compounds of arsenic. Nicotine has also been used since the late eighteenth century. There are now two main groups of synthetic insecticides.

Organochlorines

Organochlorines include DDT, Aldrin, Dieldrin and BHC. They are cheap to produce, potent and persistent. DDT was used on a massive scale from the 1930s, with a peak of 72,000 tonnes used 1970. Then usage fell as the harmful environmental effects were realized. It was found worldwide in fish and birds and was even discovered in the snow in the Antarctic. It is only slightly soluble in water but is very soluble in the bloodstream. It affects the nervous and endocrine systems and causes the eggshells of birds to lack calcium causing them to be easily breakable. It is thought to be responsible for the decline of the numbers of birds of prey like ospreys and peregrine falcons in the 1950s - they are now recovering.

As well as increased concentration via the food chain, it is known to enter via permeable membranes, so fish get it through their gills. As it has low water solubility, it tends to stay at the water surface, so organisms that live there are most affected. DDT found in fish that formed part of the human food chain caused concern, but the levels found in the liver, kidney and brain tissues was less than 1ppm and in fat was 10 ppm which was below the level likely to cause harm. However, DDT was banned in Britain and America to stop the further build up of it in the food chain. The USA exploited this ban and sold DDT to developing countries, who could not afford the expensive replacement chemicals and who did not have such stringent regulations governing the use of pesticides.

Some insects have developed a resistance to insecticides - e.g. the which carries malaria.

Organophosphates

Organophosphates, e.g. parathion, methyl parathion and about 40 other insecticides are available nationally. Parathion is highly toxic, methyl-parathion is less so and Malathion is generally considered safe as it has low toxicity and is rapidly broken down in the mammalian liver. This group works by preventing normal nerve transmission as cholinesterase is prevented from breaking down the transmitter substance acetylcholine, resulting in uncontrolled muscle movements. of a variety of pesticides into our water supplies causes concern to environmental groups, as in many cases the long term effects of these specific chemicals is not known.

Restrictions came into force in July 1985 and were so frequently broken that in 1987, formal proceedings were taken against the British government. Britain is still the only European state to use Aldrin and organochlorines, although it was supposed to stop in 1993. East Anglia has the worst record for pesticide contamination of drinking water. Of the 350 pesticides used in Britain, only 50 can be analyzed, which is worrying for the global community.

Burial

Burial is the technique used by Jews, Muslims, Christians and other religions with Abrahamic influence, to dispose off the corpse of dead humans and animals. This process leads to regular soil erosion due to loosening of soil. Also, the decomposing fluids act as poisonous herbicides, pesticides and may even lead to epidemics in surrounding areas. It leads to soil pollution, soil erosion and even water pollution.

CHAPTER–15

Soil Conservation

INTRODUCTION

Fudging is set of management strategies for prevention of soil being eroded from the earth's surface or becoming chemically altered by overuse, salinization, acidification, or other chemical soil contamination. The principal approaches these strategies take are:

- choice of vegetative cover;
- erosion prevention;
- salinity management;
- acidity control;
- encouraging health of beneficial soil organisms;
- prevention and remediation of soil contamination; and
- mineralization;

Other ways are:

- no till farming;
- contour plowing;
- wind rows;
- crop rotation;
- the use of natural and man-made fertilizer; and
- resting the land.

Many scientific disciplines are involved in these pursuits, including agronomy, hydrology, soil science, meteorology, microbiology, and environmental chemistry.

Decisions regarding appropriate crop rotation, cover crops, and planted windbreaks are central to the ability of surface soils to retain their integrity, both with respect to erosive forces and chemical change from nutrient depletion. Crop rotation is simply the conventional alternation of crops on a given field, so that nutrient depletion is avoided from repetitive chemical uptake/ deposition of single crop growth.

Cover crops serve the function of protecting the soil from erosion, weed establishment or excess evapotranspiration; however, they may also serve vital soil chemistry functions. For example, legumes can be ploughed under to augment soil nitrates, and other plants have the ability to metabolize soil contaminants or alter adverse pH. The cover crop Mucuna pruriens (velvet bean) has been used in Nigeria to increase phosphorus availability after application of rock phosphate. Some of these same precepts are applicable to urban landscaping, especially with respect to ground-cover selection for erosion control and weed suppression.

Erosion barriers on disturbed slope, Marin County, CaliforniaWindbreaks are created by planting sufficiently dense rows or stands of trees at the windward exposure of an agricultural field subject to wind erosion. Evergreen species are preferred to achieve year round protection; however, as long as foliage is present in the seasons of bare soil surfaces, the effect of deciduous trees may also be adequate. Trees, shrubs and groundcovers are also effective perimeter treatment for soil erosion prevention, by insuring any surface flows are impeded. A special form of this perimeter or inter-row treatment is the use of a "grassway" that both channels and dissipates runoff through surface friction, impeding surface runoff, and encouraging infiltration of the slowed surface water.

Erosion Prevention

Erosion

When surface planting is not feasible, there are a variety of mechanical management tactics to protect surface soils from water and wind erosion. Need for these tools arises on construction sites and other situations of transition, where bare soils are exposed. The primary tactics applied are mulching of soil surfaces and use of surface runoff barriers. From 1990 to 2005 considerable innovation has occurred in manufacture of plastic confined hay-bale products, so that a variety of shapes and sizes of runoff barriers can be delivered to the construction site.

There are also conventional practices that farmers have invoked for centuries. These fall into two main categories: contour farming and terracing, standard methods recommended by the U.S. Natural Resources Conservation Service, whose Code 330 is the common standard. Contour farming was practiced by the ancient Phoenicians, and is known to be effective for slopes between two and ten per cent Contour plowing can increase crop yields from 10 to 50 per cent, partially as a result from greater soil retention

There are many erosion control methods that can be used such as conservation tillage systems and crop rotation.

Terraced potato farming on Taquile Island, Peru.Keyline design is an enhancement of contour farming, where the total watershed properties are taken into account in forming the contour lines. Terracing is the practice of creating benches or nearly level layers on a hillside setting. Terraced farming is more common on small farms and in underdeveloped countries, since mechanized equipment is difficult to deploy in this setting.

Human overpopulation is leading to destruction of tropical forests due to widening practices of slash-and-burn and other methods of subsistence farming necessitated by famines in lesser developed countries. A sequel to the deforestation is typically large scale erosion, loss of soil nutrients and sometimes total desertification.

SALINITY MANAGEMENT

The ions responsible for salination are: Na^+, K^+, Ca_2^+, Mg_2^+ and Cl^-. Salinity is estimated to affect about one third of all the earth's arable land. Soil salinity adversely affects the metabolism of most crops, and erosion effects usually follow vegetation failure. Salinity occurs on drylands from overirrigation and in areas with shallow saline water tables. In the case of over-irrigation, salts are deposited in upper soil layers as a byproduct of most soil infiltration; excessive irrigation merely increases the rate of salt deposition. The best-known case of shallow saline water table capillary action occurred in Egypt after the 1970 construction of the Aswan Dam. The change in the groundwater level due to dam construction led to high concentration of salts in the water table. After the construction, the continuous high level of the water table led to soil salination of previously arable land.

Salt deposits on the former bed of the Aral SeaUse of humic acids may prevent excess salination, especially in locales where excessive irrigation was practiced. The mechanism involved is that humic acids can fix both anions and cations and eliminate them from root zones. In some cases it may be valuable to find plants that can tolerate saline conditions to use as surface cover until salinity can be reduced; there are a number of such saline-tolerant plants, such as saltbush, a plant found in much of North America and in the Mediterranean regions of Europe.

Soil pH

Soil pH levels adverse to crop growth can occur naturally in some regions; it can also be induced by acid rain or soil contamination from acids or bases. The role of soil pH is to control nutrient availability to vegetation. The principal macronutrients (calcium, phosphorus, nitrogen, potassium, magnesium, sulfur) prefer neutral to slightly alkaline soils. Calcium, magnesium and potassium are usually made available to plants via cation exchange surfaces of organic material and clay soil surface particles. While acidification increases the initial availability of these cations, the residual soil moisture concentrations of nutrient cations can fall to alarmingly low levels after initial nutrient uptake. Moreover, there is no simple relationship of pH to nutrient availability because of the complex combination of soil types, soil moisture regimes and meteorological factors.

The important observation is that pH is the regulatory mechanism to plant nutrient uptake, and that the theoretical concentration of soil nutrients is meaningless until pH levels are in the optimum range for uptake. Soil pH can be raised by amendment by agricultural lime; The pH of an alkaline soil is lowered by adding sulfur, iron sulfate or aluminium sulfate, although these tend to provide costly short term benefits. Urea, urea phosphate, ammonium nitrate, ammonium phosphates, ammonium sulfate and monopotassium phosphate also reduce soil pH.

SOIL ORGANISMS

Promoting the viability of beneficial soil organisms is an element of soil conservation; moreover this includes macroscopic species, notably the earthworm, as well as microorganisms. Positive effects of the earthworm are known well, as to aeration and promotion of macronutrient availability. When worms excrete egesta in the form of casts, a balanced selection of minerals and plant nutrients is made into a form accessible for root uptake. US research shows that earthworm casts are five times richer in available nitrogen, seven times richer in available phosphates and eleven times richer in available potash than the surrounding upper150 mm of soil. The weight of casts produced may be greater than 4.5 kg per worm per year. By burrowing, the earthworm is of value in creating soil porosity, creating channels enhancing the processes of aeration and drainage.

Yellow fungus, a mushroom that assists in organic decay.

This content has an uncertain copyright status and is pending deletion. You can comment on its removal.Soil microorganisms play a vital role in macronutrient wildlife. For example, nitrogen fixation is carried out by free-living or symbiotic bacteria. These bacteria have the nitrogenase enzyme that combines gaseous nitrogen with hydrogen to produce ammonia, which is then further converted by the bacteria to make other organic compounds. Some nitrogen fixing bacteria such as rhizobia live in the root nodules of legumes. Here they form a mutualistic relationship with the plant, producing ammonia in exchange for carbohydrates. In the case of the carbon cycle, carbon is transferred within the biosphere as heterotrophs feed on other organisms. This process includes the uptake of dead organic material (detritus) by fungi and bacteria in the form of fermentation or decay phenomena.

Mycorrhizae are symbiotic associations between soil-dwelling fungi and the roots of vascular plants. The mycorrhizal fungi increase the availability of minerals, water, and organic nutrients to the plant, while extracting sugars and amino acids from the plant. There are two main types, endomycorrhizae (which penetrate the roots) and ectomycorrhizae (which resemble 'socks', forming a sheath around the roots). They were discovered when scientists observed that certain seedlings failed to grow or prosper without soil from their native environment.

Some soil microorganisms known as extremophiles have remarkable properties of adaptation to extreme environmental conditions including temperature, pH and water deprivation.

The viability of soil organisms can be compromised when insecticides and herbicides are applied to planting regimes. Often there are unforeseen and unintended consequences of such chemical use in the form of death of impaired functioning of soil organisms. Thus any use of pesticides should only be undertaken after thorough understanding of residual toxicities upon soil organisms as well as terrestrial ecological components.

Killing soil microorganisms is a deleterious impact of slash and burn agricultural methods. With the surface temperatures generated, virtual annilation of soil and vegetative cover organisms are destroyed, and in many environments these effects can be virtually irreversible (at least for generations of mankind). Shifting cultivation is also a farming system that often employs slash and burn as one of its elements.

SOIL CONTAMINATION

There are thousands of roces chemicals that enter soil systems, most of which have an adverse effect upon soil quality and plant metabolism. While the role of pH has been discussed above, heavy metals, solvents, petroleum hydrocarbons, herbicides and pesticides also contribute soil residues that are of potential concern. Some of these chemicals are totally extraneous to the agricultural landscape, but others (notably herbicides and pesticides) are intentionally introduced to serve a short term function. Many of these added chemicals have long half-lives in soil, and others degrade to produce derivative chemicals that may be either persistent or pernicious.

Typically the expense of soil contamination remediation cannot be justified in an agricultural economic analysis, since cleanup costs are generally quite high; often remediation is mandated by state and county environmental health agencies based upon human health risk issues.

MINERALIZATION

To allow plants full realization of their phytonutrient potential, active mineralization of the soil is sometimes undertaken. This can be in the natural form of adding crushed rock or can take the form of chemical soil supplement. In either case the purpose is to combat mineral depletion of the soil. There are a broad range of minerals that can be added including common substances such as phosphorus and more exotic substances such as zinc and selenium. There is extensive research on the phase transitions of minerals in soil with aqueous contac

The process of flooding can bring significant bedload sediment to an alluvial plain. While this effect may not be desirable if floods endanger life or if the eroded sediment originates from productive land, this process of addition to a floodplain is a natural process that can rejuvenate soil chemistry through mineralization and macronutrient addition.

SOILS RETROGRESSION AND DEGRADATION

Soils retrogression and degradation in the French school of pedology are two regressive evolution processes associated with the loss of equilibrium of a stable soil. Retrogression is primarily due to erosion and corresponds to a phenomenon where succession reverts back to pioneer conditions (such as bare ground). Degradation is an evolution, different of natural evolution, related to the locale climate and vegetation. It is due to the replacement of the primitive vegetation (known as climax) by a secondary vegetation. This replacement modifies the humus composition and amount, and impacts the formation of the soil. It is directly related to human activity.

The soil represents the surface layer of the earth's crust.

At the beginning of a soil formation, only the bare rock outcrops. It is gradually colonized by pioneer species (lichens and mosses), then herbaceous vegetation, shrubs and finally forest. In parallel a first humus-bearing horizon is formed (the A horizon), followed by some mineral horizons (B horizons). Each successive stage is characterized by a certain association of soil/vegetation and environment, which defines an ecosystem.

After a certain time of parallel evolution between the ground and the vegetation, a state of steady balance is reached; this stage of development is called climax by some ecologists and "natural potential" by others. Succession is the evolution towards climax. Regardless of its name, the equilibrium stage of primary succession is the highest natural form of development that the environmental factors are capable of producing.

The cycles of evolution of soils have very variable durations, between a thousand-year-old for soils of quick evolution (A horizon only) to more than a million of years for soils of slow development. The same soil may achieve several successive steady state conditions during its existence, as exhibited by the Pygmy forest sequence in Mendocino County, California. Soils naturally reach a state of high productivity from which they naturally degrade as mineral nutrients are removed from the soil system. Thus older soils are more vulnerable to the effects of induced retrogression and degradation.

ECOLOGICAL FACTORS INFLUENCING SOIL FORMATION

There are two types of ecological factors influencing the evolution of a soil (through alteration and humification). These two factors are extremely significant to explain the evolution of soils of short development.

A first type of factor is the average climate of an area and the vegetation which is associated (biome). This factor allows one to define the world major areas of vegetation and soils.

A second type of factor is more local, and is related to the original rock and local drainage. This type of factor explains appearance of specialised associations (ex peat bogs).

Biorhexistasy Theory

The destruction of the vegetation implies the destruction of evoluted soils, or a regressive evolution. Cycles of succession-regression of soils follow one another within short intervals of time (human actions) or long intervals of time (climate variations).

The climate role in the deterioration of the rocks and the formation of soils lead to the formulation of the theory of the biorhexistasy.

In wet climate, the conditions are favorable to the deterioration of the rocks (mostly chemically), the development of the vegetation and the formation of soils; this period favorable to life is called biostasy.

In dry climate, the rocks exposed are mostly subjected to mechanical disintegration which produces coarse detrital materials: this is referred to as rhexistasy.

Perturbations of the Balance of a Soil

When the state of balance, characterized by the ecosystem climax is reached, it tends to be maintained stable in the course of time. The vegetation installed on the ground provides the humus and ensures the ascending circulation of the matters. It protects the ground from erosion by playing the role of barrier (for example, protection from water and wind). Plants can also reduce erosion by binding the particles of the ground to their roots.

A disturbance of climax will cause retrogression, but, if given the opportunity, nature will make every effort to restore the damage via secondary succession. Secondary succession is much faster than primary because the soil is already formed, although deteriorated and needing restoration as well.

However, when a significant destruction of the vegetation takes place (of natural origin such as an avalanche or human origin), the disturbance undergone by the ecosystem is too important. In this latter case, erosion is responsible for the destruction of the upper horizons of the ground, and is at the origin of a phenomenon of reversion to pioneer conditions. The phenomenon is called retrogression and can be partial or total (in this case, nothing remains beside bare rock). For example, the clearing of an inclined ground, subjected to violent rains, can lead to the complete destruction of the soil. Man can deeply modify the evolution of the soils by direct and brutal action, such as clearing, abusive cuts, forest pasture, litters raking. The climax vegetation is gradually replaced and the soil modified (example: replacement of leafy tree forests by moors or pines plantations). Retrogression is often related to very old human practices.

Influence of Human Activity

Erosion is the main factor for soil degradation and is due to several mechanisms: water erosion, wind erosion, chemical degradation and physical degradation.

Erosion is strongly related to human activity. For example, roads which increase impermeable surfaces lead to streaming and ground loss. Agriculture also accelerates soil erosion (increase of field size, correlated to hedges and ditches removal). Meadows are in regression to the profit of plowed lands. Spring cultures (sunflower, corn, beet) surfaces are increasing and leave the ground naked in winter. Sloping grounds are gradually colonized by vine. Lastly, use of herbicides leaves the ground naked between each crop. New cultural practices, such as mechanization also increases the risks of erosion. Fertilization by mineral manures rather than organic manure gradually destructure the soil. Many scientists observed a gradual decrease of soil organic matter content in soils, as well as a decrease of soil biological activity (in particular, in relation to chemical uses). Lastly, deforestation, in particular, is responsible for degradation of forest soils.

Agriculture increases the risk of erosion through its disturbance of vegetation by way of:

- overgrazing of animals;
- planting of a monoculture;
- row cropping;
- tilling or plowing;

- crop removal;
- land-use conversion; and
- Consequences of soil regression and degradation.

Yields impact: Recent increases in the human population have placed a great strain on the world's soil systems. More than 6 billion people are now using about 38% of the land area of the Earth to raise crops and livestock. Many soils suffer from various types of degradation, that can ultimately reduce their ability to produce food resources. Slight degradation refers to land where yield potential has been reduced by 10%, moderate degradation refers to a yield decrease from 10-50 %. Severely degraded soils have lost more than 50% of their potential. Most severely degraded soils are located in developing countries such as Asia and Africa.

Deterioration of the water quality: The increase in the turbidity of water and the contribution of nitrogen and of phosphorus can result in eutrophication. Soils particles in surface waters are also accompanied by agricultural inputs and by some pollutants of industrial, urban and road origin (such as heavy metals). The ecological impact of agricultural inputs (such as weed killer) is known but difficult to evaluate because of the multiplicity of the products and their broad spectrum of action.

Biological diversity: soil degradation may involve the disappearance of the climax vegetation, the decrease in animal habitat, thus leading to a biodiversity loss and animal extinction.

SOIL ENHANCEMENT AND REBUILDING

Problems of soil erosion can be fought, and certain practices can lead to soil enhancement and rebuilding. Even though simple, methods for reducing erosion are often not chosen because these practices outweigh the short-term benefits. Rebuilding is especially possible through the improvement of soil structure, addition of organic matter and limitation of runoff. However, these techniques will never totally succeed to restore a soil (and the fauna and flora associated to it) that took more than 1000 years to build up.

Index